SOUTHERN
Regional R

C000178846

CONTENTS

REFERENCE

MOTORWAY	**M3**
Under Construction	
Proposed	
MOTORWAY JUNCTIONS WITH NUMBERS	
Unlimited interchange **4** Limited interchange **5**	
MOTORWAY SERVICE AREA	**ROWNHAMS** Ⓢ
with access from one carriageway only	Ⓢ
MAJOR ROAD SERVICE AREAS	**SUTTON SCOTNEY**
with 24 hour Facilities	Ⓢ
PRIMARY ROUTE	**A33**
PRIMARY ROUTE DESTINATION	**POOLE**
DUAL CARRIAGEWAYS (A & B Roads)	
CLASS A ROAD	**A30**
CLASS B ROAD	**B2070**
MAJOR ROADS UNDER CONSTRUCTION	
MAJOR ROADS PROPOSED	
SAFETY CAMERAS WITH SPEED LIMITS	
Single Camera	(30)
Multiple Cameras located along road	(50)
Single & Multiple Variable Speed Cameras	(V) (V)
GRADIENT 1:5(20%) & STEEPER (Ascent in direction of arrow)	«
TOLL	**TOLL**
MILEAGE BETWEEN MARKERS	8
RAILWAY AND STATION	
LEVEL CROSSING AND TUNNEL	
RIVER OR CANAL	
COUNTY OR UNITARY AUTHORITY BOUNDARY	- + -
NATIONAL BOUNDARY	- + - + -
BUILT-UP AREA	
VILLAGE OR HAMLET	
WOODED AREA	
SPOT HEIGHT IN FEET	• 813
HEIGHT ABOVE SEA LEVEL	400' - 1,000' 122m - 305m
	1,000' - 1,400' 305m - 427m
	1,400' - 2,000' 427m - 610m
	2,000' + 610m +
NATIONAL GRID REFERENCE (Kilometres)	100
AREA COVERED BY TOWN PLAN	**SEE PAGE 55**

TOURIST INFORMATION

AIRPORT	✈
AIRFIELD	✛
HELIPORT	
BATTLE SITE AND DATE	⚔ *1066*
CASTLE (Open to Public)	
CASTLE WITH GARDEN (Open to Public)	
CATHEDRAL, ABBEY, CHURCH, FRIARY, PRIORY	✝
COUNTRY PARK	
FERRY (Vehicular)	
(Foot only)	
GARDEN (Open to Public)	
GOLF COURSE _____ 9 HOLE ___ 🏴 18 HOLE	🏴18
HISTORIC BUILDING (Open to Public)	
HISTORIC BUILDING WITH GARDEN (Open to Public)	
HORSE RACECOURSE	
INFORMATION CENTRE	🛈
LIGHTHOUSE	
MOTOR RACING CIRCUIT	
MUSEUM, ART GALLERY	
NATIONAL PARK OR FOREST PARK	
NATIONAL TRUST PROPERTY (Open)	*NT*
(Restricted Opening)	*NT*
NATURE RESERVE OR BIRD SANCTUARY	
NATURE TRAIL OR FOREST WALK	
PLACE OF INTEREST	*Monument* •
PICNIC SITE	
RAILWAY, STEAM OR NARROW GAUGE	
THEME PARK	
VIEWPOINT _____ 360 degrees	
180 degrees	
VISITOR CENTRE	
WILDLIFE PARK	
WINDMILL	
ZOO OR SAFARI PARK	

SCALE

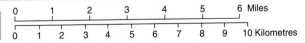

0   1   2   3   4   5   6 Miles
0   1   2   3   4   5   6   7   8   9   10 Kilometres

1:158,400
2.5 Miles to 1 Inch

Geographers' A-Z Map Company Ltd
Fairfield Road, Borough Green,
Sevenoaks, Kent TN15 8PP
01732 781000 (Enquiries & Trade Sales)
01732 783422 (Retail Sales)
www.a-zmaps.co.uk
Edition 10 2009
Copyright © Geographers' A-Z Map Company Ltd.

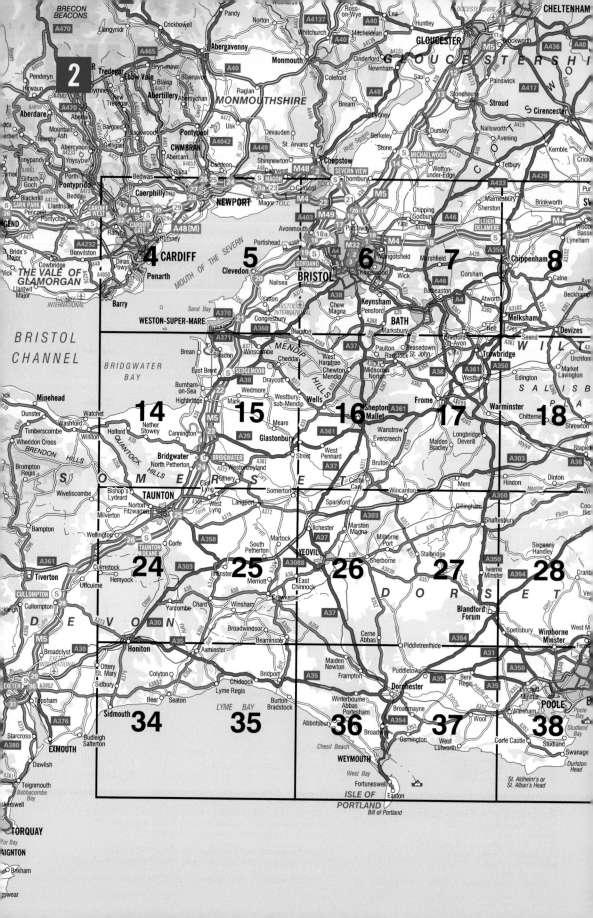

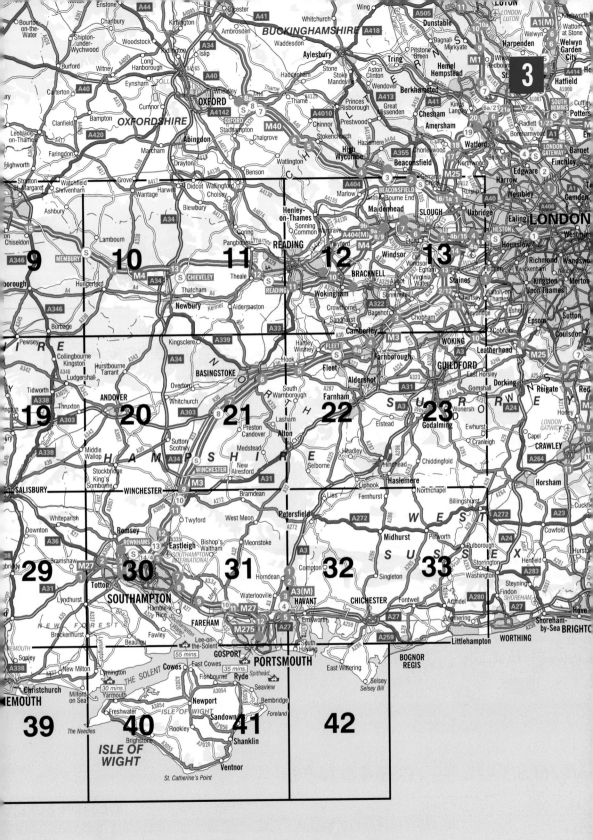

ENGLISH CHANNEL

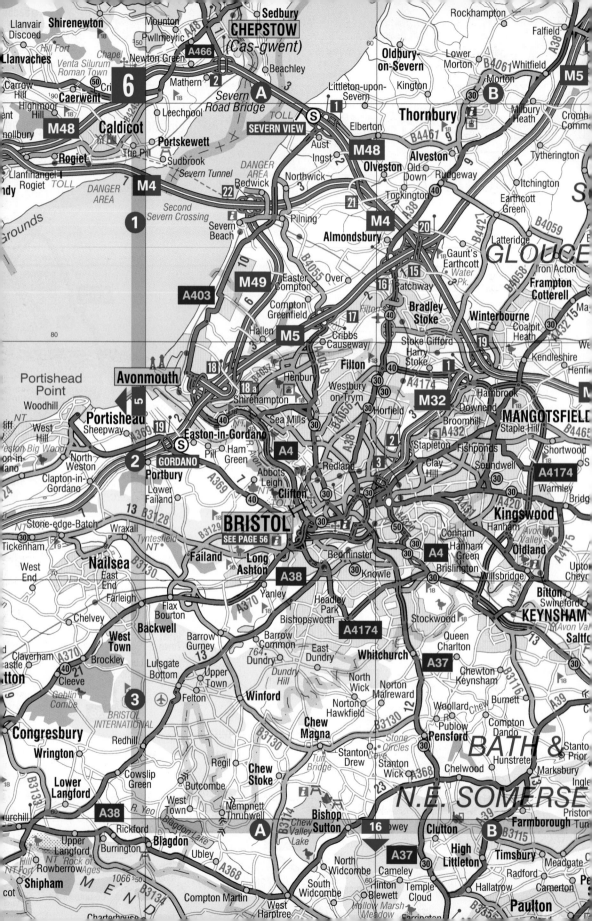

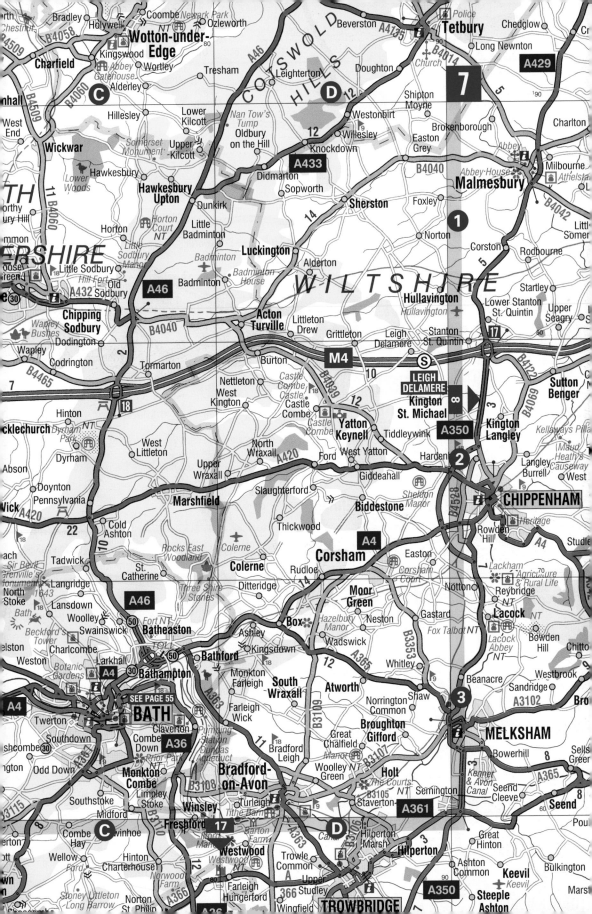

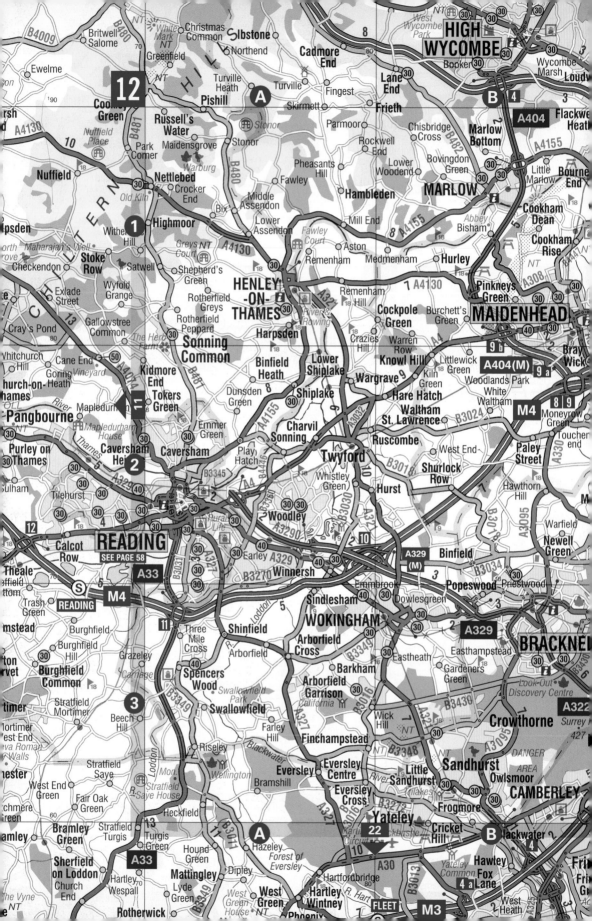

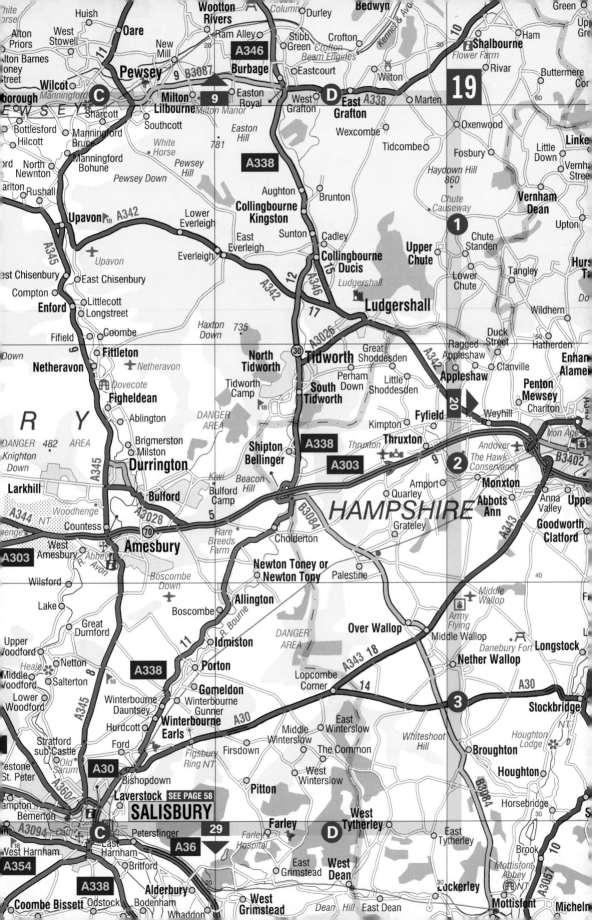

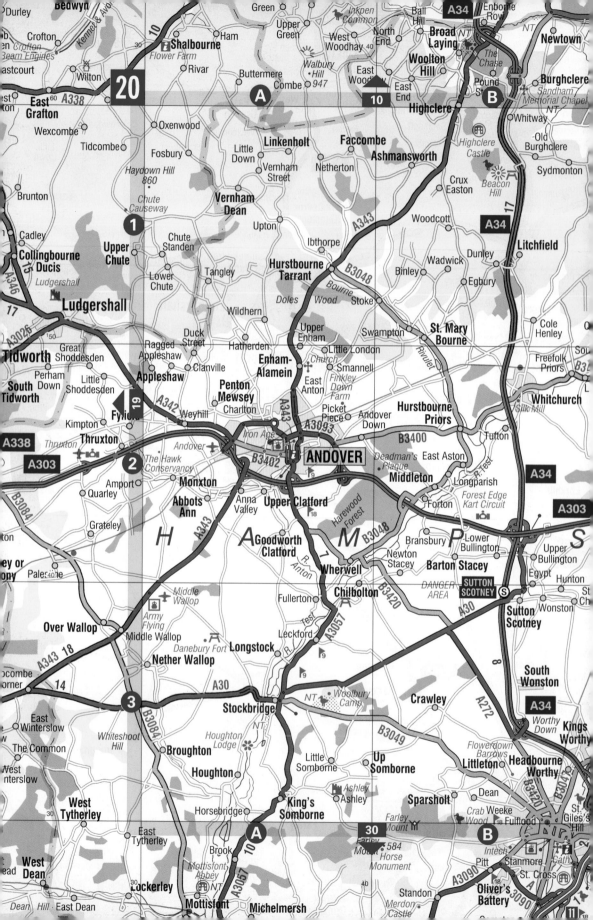

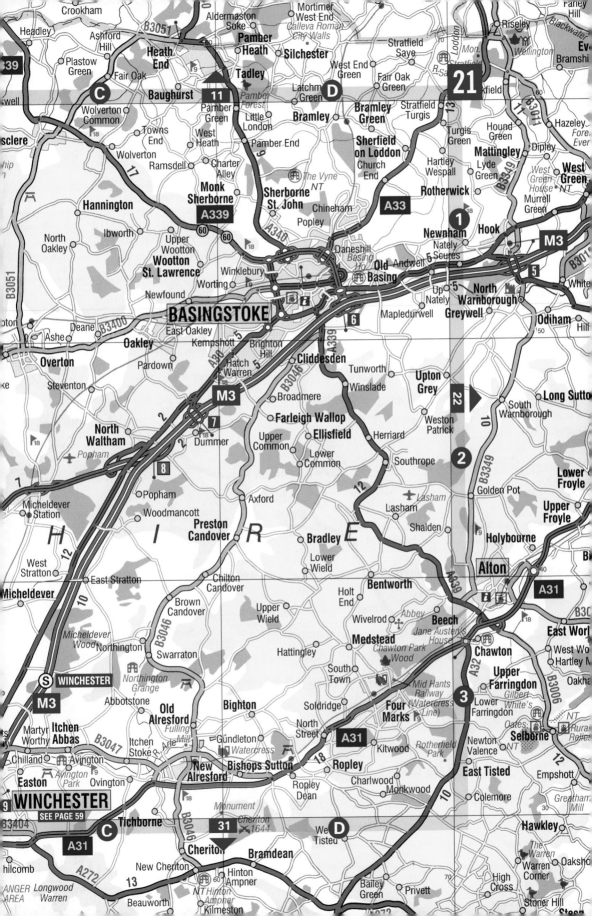

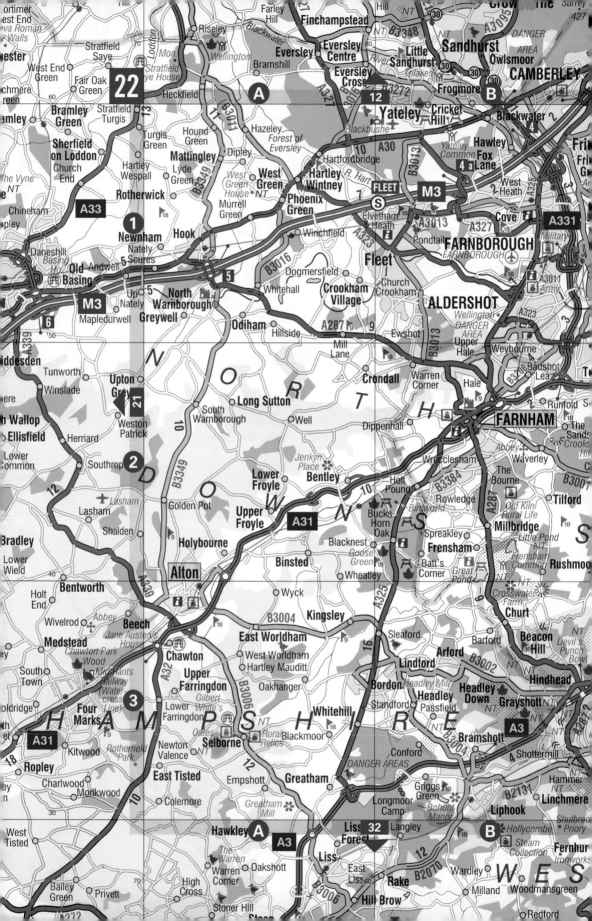

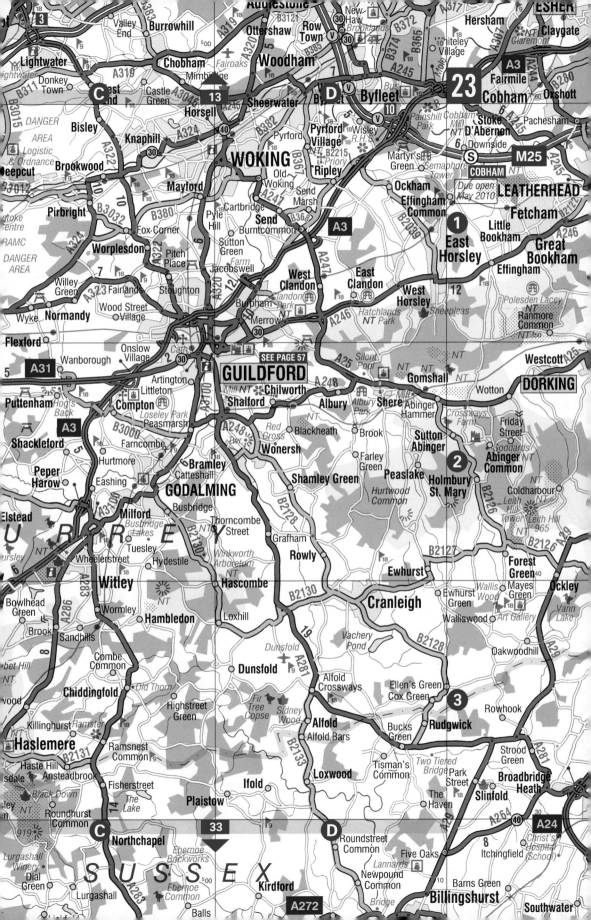

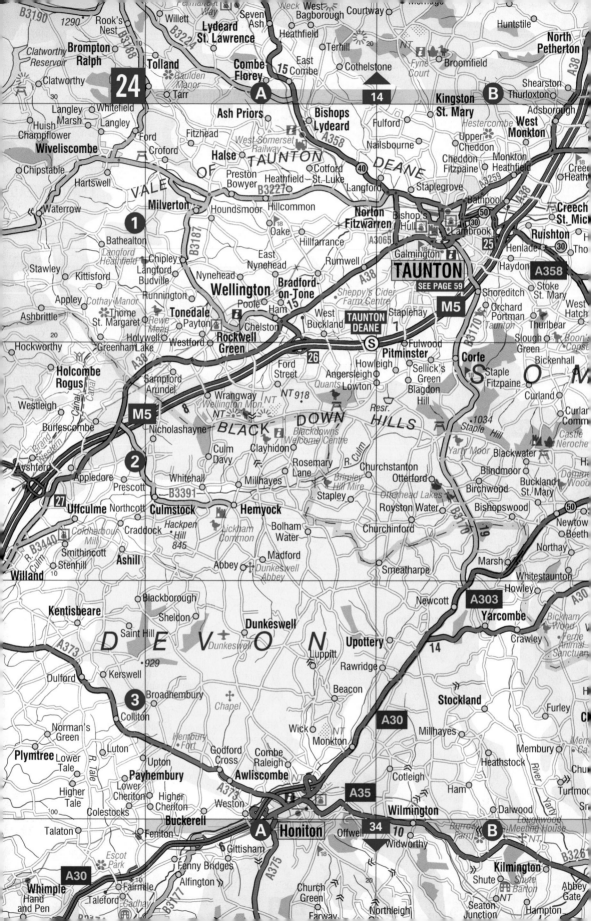

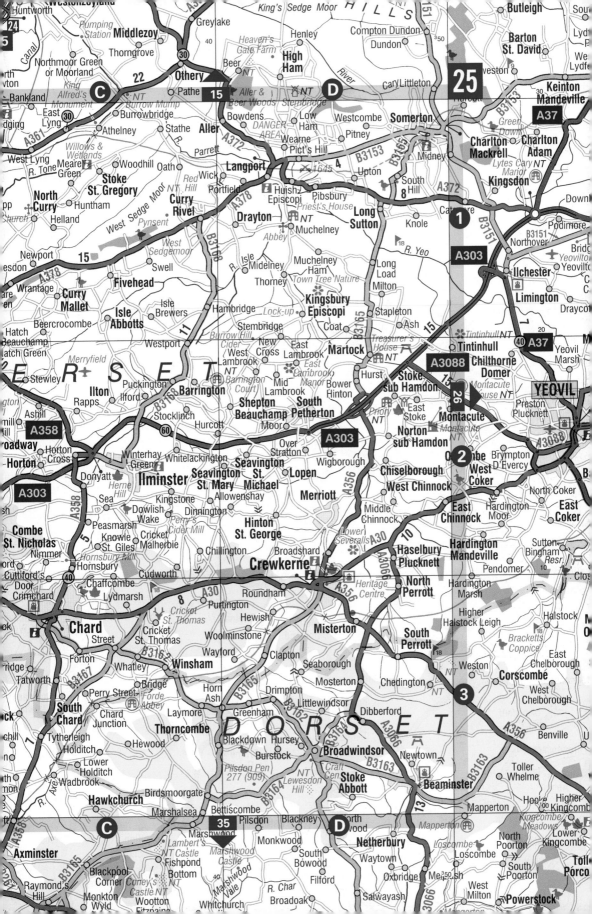

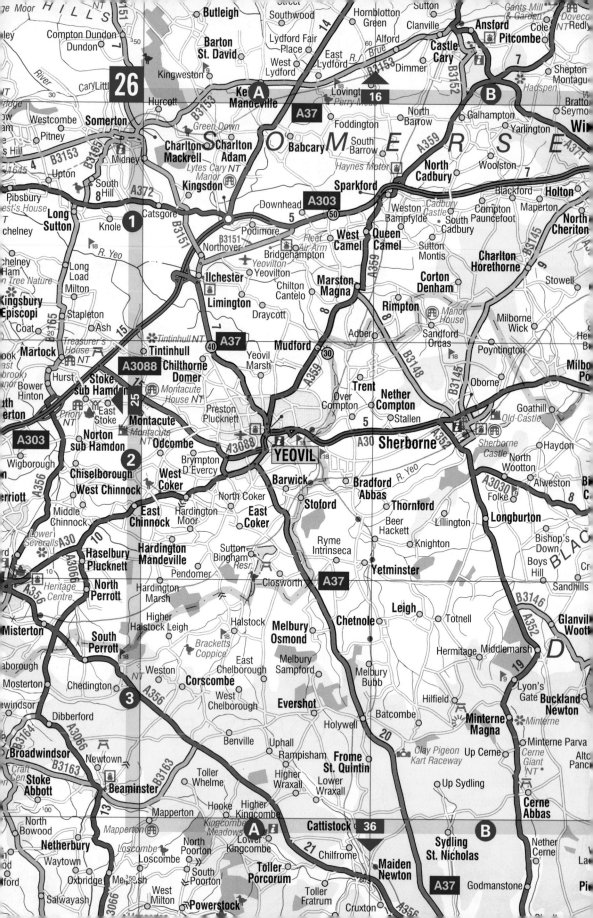

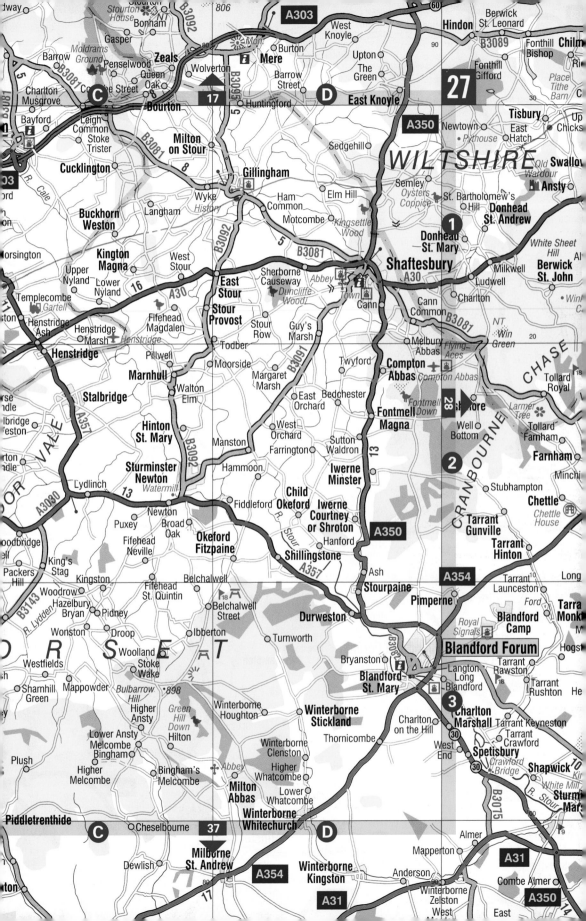

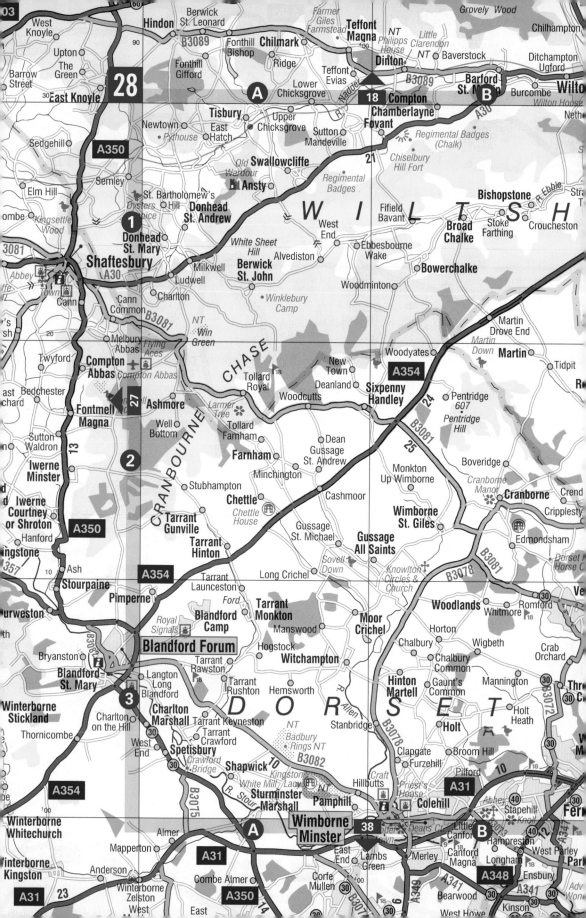

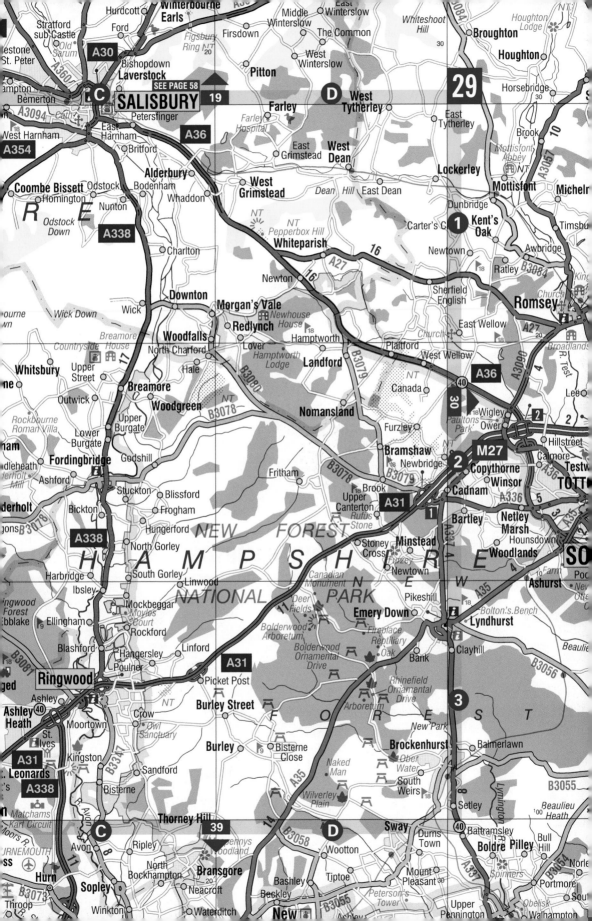

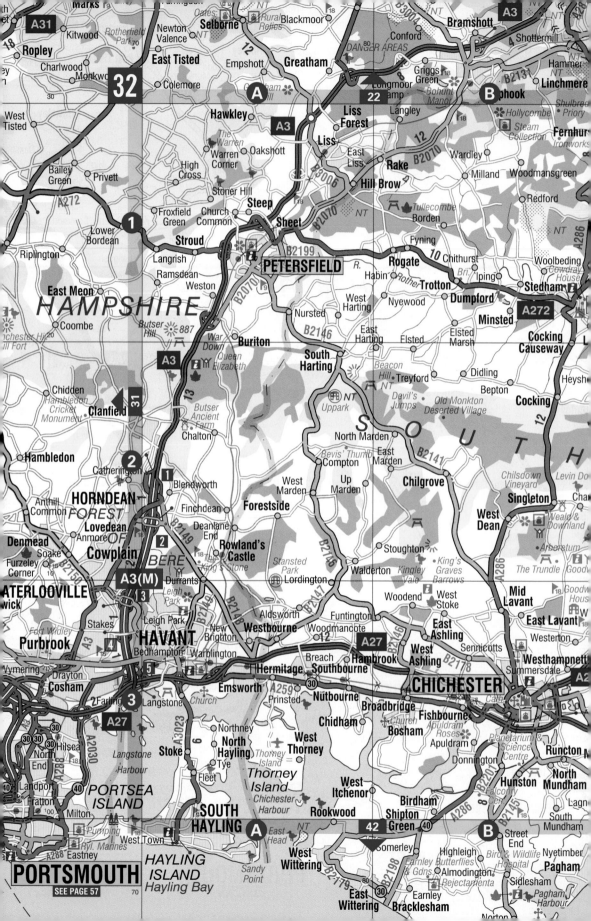

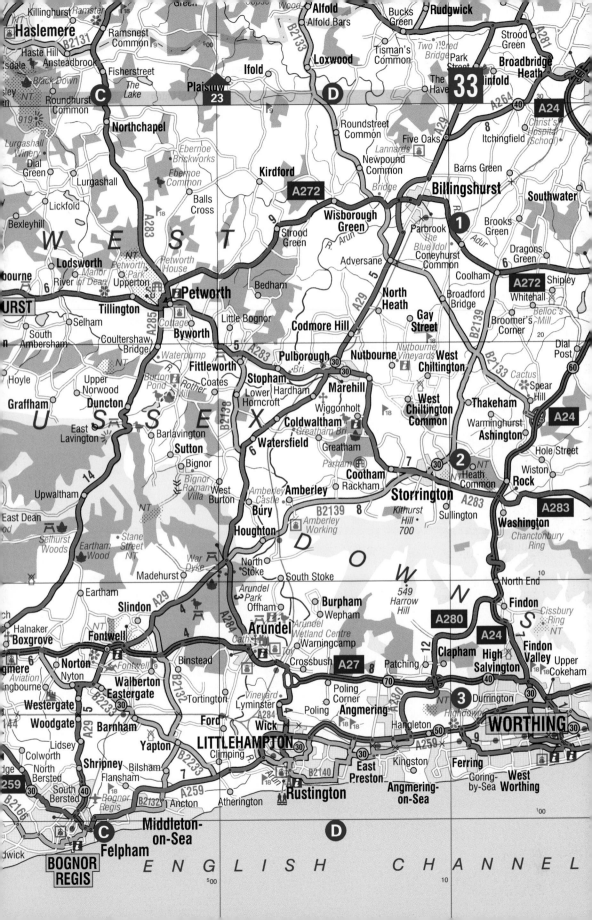

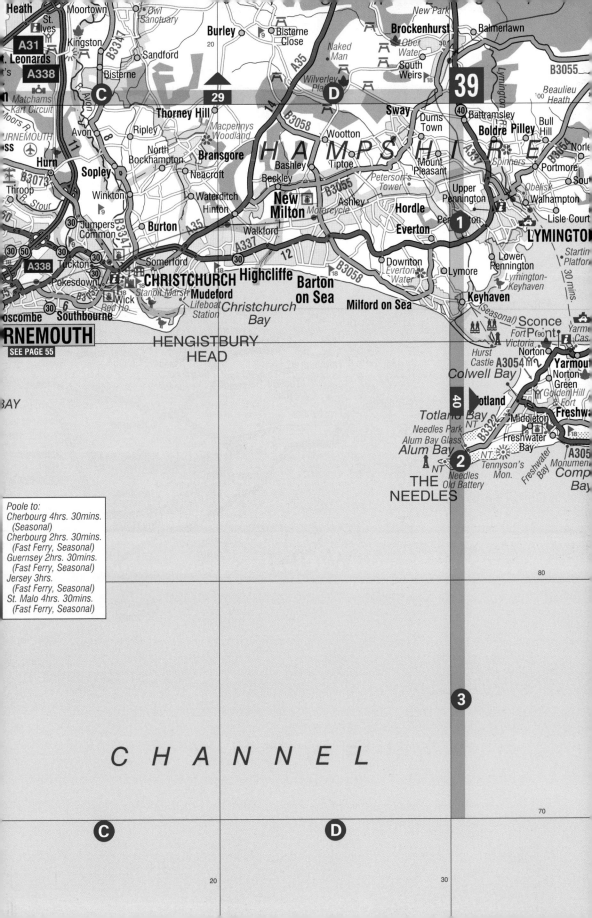

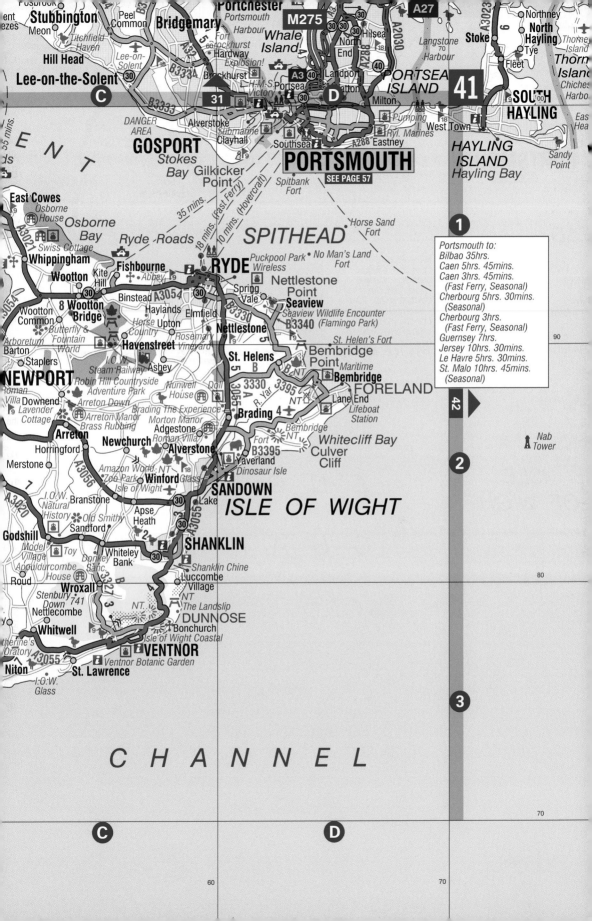

Isle of Wight map (Page 41)

Stubbington
Meon
Bridgemary
Peel Common
Portchester
Portsmouth Harbour
M275
A27
A3023
Northney
North Hayling
Stoke
6
Tye
Fleet
Thorne Island
Thorn Island
Whale Island
North End
Hilsea
A2030
Langstone Harbour
70
Chiches Harbo
Hill Head
Titchfield Haven
Lee-on-Solent
Fort Rockhurst
Hardway
Explosion!
H.M.S. Victory
A3
Landport
Fratton
A288
PORTSEA ISLAND
Milton
SOUTH HAYLING
West Town
Eas Hea
Lee-on-the-Solent
C
B3334
Brockhurst
31
D
Pumping
Ryl. Marines
Eastney
41
Alverstoke
Clayhall
Southsea
Submarine
A288
HAYLING ISLAND
Hayling Bay
GOSPORT
Stokes Bay
Gilkicker Point
PORTSMOUTH
SEE PAGE 57
Spitbank Fort
Sandy Point

DANGER AREA

East Cowes
Osborne House
Osborne Bay
Ryde Roads
35 mins. (Fast Ferry)
18 mins. (Fast Ferry)
10 mins. (Hovercraft)
Horse Sand Fort
SPITHEAD
No Man's Land Fort
1
A3021
Swiss Cottage
Whippingham
Wootton
Kite Hill
Fishbourne
Abbey
RYDE
Puckpool Park
Wireless
Nettlestone Point
Seaview
Seaview Wildlife Encounter (Flamingo Park)
Horse Sand Fort

Portsmouth to:
Bilbao 35hrs.
Caen 5hrs. 45mins.
Caen 3hrs. 45mins.
(Fast Ferry, Seasonal)
Cherbourg 5hrs. 30mins.
(Seasonal)
Cherbourg 3hrs.
(Fast Ferry, Seasonal)
Guernsey 7hrs.
Jersey 10hrs. 30mins.
Le Havre 5hrs. 30mins.
St. Malo 10hrs. 45mins.
(Seasonal)

90

8 Wootton Bridge
Binstead
A3054
Spring Vale
B3330
B3340
Wootton Common
Horse Country
Upton
Elmfield
Nettlestone
Rosemary Vineyard
St. Helen's Fort
Butterfly & Fountain World
Arboretum
Barton
Staplers
I.O.W. Steam Railway
Havenstreet
Ashey
St. Helens
Bembridge Point
Bembridge
Maritime
FORELAND
42
NEWPORT
Downend
Roman Villa
Lavender Cottage
Robin Hill Countryside Adventure Park
Arreton Down
Nunwell House
Doll
Brading The Experience
3330
R. Yar
3395
Lane End
Lifeboat Station
Nab Tower
Arreton
Arreton Manor Brass Rubbing
Morton Manor
Adgestone
Roman Villa
Brading
Fort
Bembridge
NT
Whitecliff Bay
Culver Cliff
2
Horringford
Merstone
Newchurch
Alverstone
Yaverland
B3395
Amazon World: NT
Zoo Park
Winford
Dinosaur Isle
Glass
A3056
I.O.W. Natural History
Branstone
18
Lake
SANDOWN
ISLE OF WIGHT
A3020
7
Old Smithy
Apse Heath
30
A3055
Godshill
Model Village
Toy
Sandford
Whiteley Bank
30
SHANKLIN
80
Apuldurcombe House
Donkey Sanc.
Shanklin Chine
Luccombe
Village
Roud
B3327
3
Wroxall
NT
The Landslip
Stenbury Down 741
NT
DUNNOSE
Nettlecombe
Whitwell
Bonchurch
Isle of Wight Coastal
St. Catherine's Oratory
A3055
VENTNOR
3
Niton
St. Lawrence
Ventnor Botanic Garden
I.O.W. Glass

C H A N N E L

70

C
D

60
70

INDEX TO CITIES, TOWNS, VILLAGES, HAMLETS & LOCATIONS

(1) A strict alphabetical order is used e.g. Bishop Sutton follows Bishopstrow but precedes Bishop's Waltham.

(2) The map reference given refers to the actual map square in which the town spot or built-up area is located and not to the place name.

(3) Only one reference is given although due to page overlaps the place may appear on more than one page.

(4) Where two places of the same name occur in the same County or Unitary Authority, the nearest large town is also given;
e.g. Allington. *Wilts* . . . .3D **19** (nr. Amesbury) indicates that Allington is located in square 3D on page **19** and is situated near Amesbury in the County of Wiltshire.

(5) Major towns are shown in bold i.e. **Bath.** *Bath* . . . .3C **7** & **55.** Where they appear on a Town Plan a second page reference is given.

COUNTIES AND UNITARY AUTHORITIES with the abbreviations used in this index

Bath & N E Somerset : *Bath*
Bournemouth : *Bour*
Bracknell Forest : *Brac*
Bristol : *Bris*
Buckinghamshire : *Buck*
Caerphilly : *Cphy*
Cardiff : *Card*
Devon : *Devn*
Dorset : *Dors*
Gloucestershire : *Glos*
Greater London : *G Lon*
Hampshire : *Hants*
Hertfordshire : *Herts*
Isle of Wight : *IOW*
Monmouthshire : *Mon*
Newport : *Newp*
North Somerset : *N Som*
Oxfordshire : *Oxon*
Poole : *Pool*
Portsmouth : *Port*
Reading : *Read*
Rhondda Cynon Taff : *Rhon*
Slough : *Slo*
Somerset : *Som*
Southampton : *Sotn*
South Gloucestershire : *S Glo*
Surrey : *Surr*
Swindon : *Swin*
Torfaen : *Torf*
Vale of Glamorgan, The : *V Glam*
West Berkshire : *W Ber*
West Sussex : *W Sus*
Wiltshire : *Wilts*
Windsor & Maidenhead : *Wind*
Wokingham : *Wok*

A

Abbas Combe. *Som* 1C **27**
Abbey. *Devn* 2A **24**
Abbey Gate. *Devn* 1B **34**
Abbots Ann. *Hants* 2A **20**
Abbotsbury. *Dors* 2A **36**
Abbots Leigh. *N Som* 2A **6**
Abbotstone. *Hants* 3C **21**
Abbots Worthy. *Hants* 3B **20**
Abertridwr. *Cphy* 1A **4**
Abinger Common. *Surr* 2D **23**
Abinger Hammer. *Surr* 2D **23**
Ablington. *Wilts* 2C **19**
Abson. *S Glo* 2C **7**
Acton. *Dors* 3A **38**
Acton Turville. *S Glo* 1D **7**
Adber. *Dors* 1B **26**
Addlestone. *Surr* 3D **13**
Adgestone. *IOW* 2C **41**
Adsborough. *Som* 1B **24**
Adversane. *W Sus* 1D **33**
Affpuddle. *Dors* 1D **37**
Aisholt. *Som* 3A **14**
Albury. *Surr* 2D **23**
Aldbourne. *Wilts* 2D **9**
Alderbury. *Wilts* 1C **29**
Alderholt. *Dors* 2C **29**
Alderley. *Glos* 1C **7**
Aldermaston. *W Ber* 3C **11**
Aldermaston Stoke. *W Ber* 3D **11**
Aldermaston Wharf. *W Ber* 3D **11**
Aldershot. *Hants* 1B **22**
Alderton. *Wilts* 1D **7**
Aldingbourne. *W Sus* 3C **33**
Aldsworth. *W Sus* 3A **32**
Aldwick. *W Sus* 3C **33**
Aldworth. *W Ber* 2C **11**
Aley. *Som* 3A **14**
Alfington. *Devn* 1A **34**
Alfold. *Surr* 3D **23**
Alfold Bars. *W Sus* 3D **23**
Alfold Crossways. *Surr* 3D **23**
Alford. *Som* 3B **16**
Alhampton. *Som* 3B **16**
Allbrook. *Hants* 1B **30**
All Cannings. *Wilts* 3B **8**
Aller. *Som* 1D **25**
Allercombe. *Devn* 1A **34**
Allington. *Wilts* 3D **19**
(nr. Amesbury)
Allington. *Wilts* 3B **8**
(nr. Devizes)
Allowenshay. *Som* 2C **25**
Almer. *Dors* 1A **38**
Almodington. *W Sus* 1B **42**
Almondsbury. *S Glo* 1B **6**
Alston. *Devn* 3C **25**
Alstone. *Som* 2C **15**
Alston Sutton. *Som* 1D **15**
Alton. *Hants* 3A **22**
Alton Barnes. *Wilts* 3C **9**
Alton Pancras. *Dors* 3C **27**
Alton Priors. *Wilts* 3C **9**
Alvediston. *Wilts* 1A **28**
Alverstoke. *Hants* 1C **41**
Alverstone. *IOW* 2C **41**
Alveston. *S Glo* 1B **6**
Alweston. *Dors* 2B **26**
Amberley. *W Sus* 2D **33**
Amesbury. *Wilts* 2C **19**
Ampfield. *Hants* 1A **30**
Amport. *Hants* 2D **19**
Ancton. *W Sus* 3C **33**
Anderson. *Dors* 1D **37**
Andover. *Hants* 2A **20**
Andover Down. *Hants* 2A **20**
Andwell. *Hants* 1D **21**
Angersleigh. *Som* 2B **24**
Angmering. *W Sus* 3D **33**
Angmering-on-Sea. *W Sus* 3D **33**
Anmore. *Hants* 2D **31**
Anna Valley. *Hants* 2A **20**
Ansford. *Som* 3B **16**
Ansteadbrook. *Surr* 3C **23**
Ansty. *Wilts* 1A **28**
Anthill Common. *Hants* 2D **31**
Appledore. *Devn* 2A **24**
Appleford. *Oxon* 1C **11**
Applemore. *Hants* 3A **30**
Appleshaw. *Hants* 2A **20**
Appley. *Som* 1A **24**
Apse Heath. *IOW* 2C **41**
Apuldram. *W Sus* 3B **32**
Arborfield. *Wok* 3A **12**
Arborfield Cross. *Wok* 3A **12**
Arborfield Garrison. *Wok* 3A **12**
Ardington. *Oxon* 1B **10**
Arford. *Hants* 3B **22**
Arne. *Dors* 2A **38**
Arreton. *IOW* 2C **41**
Artington. *Surr* 2C **23**
Arundel. *W Sus* 3D **33**
Ascot. *Wind* 3C **13**
Ash. *Dors* 2D **27**
Ash. *Som* 1D **25**
Ash. *Surr* 1B **22**
Ashampstead. *W Ber* 2C **11**
Ashbrittle. *Som* 1A **24**
Ashbury. *Oxon* 1D **9**
Ashcott. *Som* 3D **15**
Ashe. *Hants* 1C **21**
Ashey. *IOW* 2C **41**
Ashfield. *Hants* 2A **30**
Ashford. *Hants* 2C **29**
Ashford. *Surr* 2D **13**
Ashford Hill. *Hants* 3C **11**
Ashill. *Devn* 2A **24**
Ashill. *Som* 2C **25**
Ashington. *W Sus* 2D **33**
Ashlett. *Hants* 3B **30**
Ashley. *Dors* 3C **29**
Ashley. *Hants* 1D **39**
(nr. New Milton)
Ashley. *Hants* 3A **20**
(nr. Winchester)
Ashley. *Wilts* 3D **7**
Ashley Heath. *Dors* 3C **29**
Ashmansworth. *Hants* 1B **20**
Ashmore. *Dors* 2A **28**
Ashmore Green. *W Ber* 3C **11**
Ash Priors. *Som* 1A **24**
Ashton Common. *Wilts* 1A **18**
Ashurst. *Hants* 2A **30**
Ash Vale. *Surr* 1B **22**
Ashwick. *Som* 2B **16**
Askerswell. *Dors* 1A **36**
Aston. *Wok* 1A **12**
Aston Tirrold. *Oxon* 1C **11**
Aston Upthorpe. *Oxon* 1C **11**
Athelhampton. *Dors* 1C **37**
Athelney. *Som* 1C **25**
Atherfield Green. *IOW* 3B **40**
Atherington. *W Sus* 3D **33**
Atworth. *Wilts* 3D **7**
Aughton. *Wilts* 1D **19**
Aust. *S Glo* 1A **6**
Avebury. *Wilts* 3C **9**
Avebury Trusloe. *Wilts* 3B **8**
Avington. *Hants* 3C **21**
Avon. *Hants* 1C **39**
Avonmouth. *Bris* 2A **6**
Awbridge. *Hants* 1A **30**
Awliscombe. *Devn* 3A **24**
Axbridge. *Som* 1D **15**
Axford. *Hants* 2D **21**
Axford. *Wilts* 3D **9**
Axminster. *Devn* 1B **34**
Axmouth. *Devn* 1B **34**
Ayshford. *Devn* 2A **24**

B

Babcary. *Som* 1A **26**
Backwell. *N Som* 3D **5**
Badbury. *Swin* 1C **9**
Badgworth. *Som* 1C **15**
Badminton. *S Glo* 1D **7**
Badshot Lea. *Surr* 2B **22**
Bagley. *Som* 2D **15**
Bagnor. *W Ber* 3B **10**
Bagshot. *Surr* 3C **13**
Bagshot. *Wilts* 3A **10**
Bagstone. *S Glo* 1B **6**
Bailey Green. *Hants* 1D **31**
Ball Hill. *Hants* 3B **10**
Balls Cross. *W Sus* 1C **33**
Balmerlawn. *Hants* 3A **30**
Baltonsborough. *Som* 3A **16**
Bank. *Hants* 3D **29**
Bankland. *Som* 1C **25**
Banwell. *N Som* 1C **15**
Bapton. *Wilts* 3A **18**
Barford. *Hants* 3B **22**
Barford St Martin. *Wilts* 3B **18**
Barkham. *Wok* 3A **12**
Barlavington. *W Sus* 2C **33**
Barnham. *W Sus* 3C **33**
Barns Green. *W Sus* 1D **33**
Barri. *V Glam* 3A **4**
Barrington. *Som* 2C **25**
Barrow. *Som* 3C **17**
Barrow Common. *N Som* 3A **6**
Barrow Gurney. *N Som* 3A **6**
Barrow Street. *Wilts* 3D **17**
Barry. *V Glam* 3A **4**
Barry Island. *V Glam* 3A **4**
Bartley. *Hants* 2A **30**
Barton. *IOW* 2C **41**
Barton. *N Som* 1C **15**
Barton on Sea. *Hants* 1D **39**
Barton St David. *Som* 3A **16**
Barton Stacey. *Hants* 2B **20**
Barwick. *Som* 2A **26**
Bashley. *Hants* 1D **39**
Basingstoke. *Hants* 1D **21**
Bason Bridge. *Som* 2C **15**
Bassaleg. *Newp* 1B **4**
Bassett. *Sotn* 2B **30**
Batchworth. *Herts* 1D **13**
Batcombe. *Dors* 3B **26**
Batcombe. *Som* 3B **16**
Bath. *Bath* . . . . .3C **7** & **55**
Bathampton. *Bath* 3C **7**
Bathealton. *Som* 1A **24**
Batheaston. *Bath* 3C **7**
Bathford. *Bath* 3C **7**
Bathpool. *Som* 1B **24**
Bathway. *Som* 1A **16**
Battleborough. *Som* 1C **15**
Battramsley. *Hants* 1A **40**
Batt's Corner. *Surr* 2B **22**
Baughurst. *Hants* 3C **11**
Baulking. *Oxon* 1A **10**
Baverstock. *Wilts* 3B **18**
Bawdrip. *Som* 3C **15**
Baybridge. *Hants* 1C **31**
Baydon. *Wilts* 2D **9**
Bayford. *Som* 1C **27**
Beach. *S Glo* 2C **7**
Beachley. *Glos* 1A **6**
Beacon. *Devn* 3A **24**
Beacon Hill. *Surr* 3B **22**
Beaconsfield. *Buck* 1C **13**
Beaminster. *Dors* 3D **25**
Beanacre. *Wilts* 3A **8**
Bearwood. *Pool* 1B **38**
Beaulieu. *Hants* 3A **30**
Beauworth. *Hants* 1C **31**
Beckhampton. *Wilts* 3B **8**
Beckington. *Som* 1D **17**
Beckley. *Hants* 1D **39**
Bedchester. *Dors* 2D **27**
Beddau. *Rhon* 1A **4**
Bedham. *W Sus* 1D **33**
Bedhampton. *Hants* 3A **32**
Bedminster. *Bris* 2A **6**
Bedwas. *Cphy* 1A **4**
Beech. *Hants* 3D **21**
Beech Hill. *W Ber* 3D **11**
Beechingstoke. *Wilts* 1B **18**
Beedon. *W Ber* 2B **10**
Beenham. *W Ber* 3C **11**
Beer. *Devn* 2B **34**
Beer. *Som* 3D **15**
Beercrocombe. *Som* 1C **25**
Beer Hackett. *Dors* 2B **26**
Beetham. *Som* 2B **24**
Began. *Card* 1B **4**
Beggearn Huish. *Som* 3A **14**
Belchalwell. *Dors* 3C **27**
Belchalwell Street. *Dors* 3C **27**
Bembridge. *IOW* 2D **41**
Bemerton. *Wilts* 3C **19**
Benson. *Oxon* 1D **11**
Bentley. *Hants* 2A **22**
Bentworth. *Hants* 2D **21**
Benville. *Dors* 3A **26**
Bepton. *W Sus* 2B **32**
Bere Regis. *Dors* 1D **37**
Berkley. *Som* 2D **17**
Berrick Salome. *Oxon* 1D **11**
Berrow. *Som* 1C **15**
Berwick Bassett. *Wilts* 2C **9**
Berwick St James. *Wilts* 3B **18**
Berwick St John. *Wilts* 1A **28**
Berwick St Leonard. *Wilts* 3A **18**
Bettiscombe. *Dors* 1D **35**
Bettws. *Newp* 1B **4**
Beverston. *Glos* 1D **7**
Bexleyhill. *W Sus* 1C **33**
Bickenhall. *Som* 2B **24**

Bicknoller—Chalfont Common

Bicknoller. *Som* 3A **14**
Bickton. *Hants* 2C **29**
Biddestone. *Wilts* 2D **7**
Biddisham. *Som* 1C **15**
Bierley. *IOW* 3C **41**
Bighton. *Hants* 3D **21**
Bignor. *W Sus* 2C **33**
Billingshurst. *W Sus* 1D **33**
Bilsham. *W Sus* 3C **33**
Bincombe. *Dors* 2B **36**
Binegar. *Som* 2B **16**
Binfield. *Brac* 2B **12**
Binfield Heath. *Oxon* 2A **12**
Bingham's Melcombe. *Dors* 3C **27**
Binley. *Hants* 1B **20**
Binnegar. *Dors* 2D **37**
Binstead. *IOW* 1C **41**
Binstead. *W Sus* 3C **33**
Binsted. *Hants* 2A **22**
Birchgrove. *Card* 2A **4**
Birchill. *Devn* 3C **25**
Birchwood. *Som* 2B **24**
Birdham. *W Sus* 3B **32**
Birdsmoorgate. *Dors* 3C **25**
Bisham. *Wind* 1B **12**
Bishopdown. *Wilts* 3C **19**
Bishops Cannings. *Wilts* 3B **8**
Bishop's Caundle. *Dors* 2B **26**
Bishop's Down. *Dors* 2B **26**
Bishop's Green. *Hants* 3C **11**
Bishop's Hull. *Som* 1B **24**
Bishops Lydeard. *Som* 1A **24**
Bishops Sutton. *Hants* 3D **21**
Bishopstoke. *Hants* 2B **30**
Bishopstone. *Swin* 1D **9**
Bishopstone. *Wilts* 1B **28**
Bishopstrow. *Wilts* 2D **17**
Bishop Sutton. *Bath* 1A **16**
Bishop's Waltham. *Hants* 2C **31**
Bishopswood. *Som* 2B **24**
Bishopsworth. *Bris* 3A **6**
Bishton. *Newp* 1C **5**
Bisley. *Surr* 1C **23**
Bisterne. *Hants* 3C **29**
Bisterne Close. *Hants* 3D **29**
Bitterne. *Sotn* 2B **30**
Bitton. *S Glo* 3B **6**
Bix. *Oxon* 1A **12**
Blackborough. *Devn* 3A **24**
Blackdown. *Dors* 3C **25**
Blackfield. *Hants* 3B **30**
Blackford. *Som* 2D **15**
(nr. Burnham-on-Sea)
Blackford. *Som* 1B **26**
(nr. Wincanton)
Blackgang. *IOW* 3B **40**
Blackheath. *Surr* 2D **23**
Blackland. *Wilts* 3B **8**
Blackmoor. *Hants* 3A **22**
Blacknest. *Hants* 2A **22**
Blackney. *Dors* 1D **35**
Blacknoll. *Dors* 2D **37**
Blackpool Corner. *Devn* 1C **35**
Blacktown. *Newp* 1B **4**
Blackwater. *Hants* 1B **22**
Blackwater. *IOW* 2C **41**
Blackwater. *Som* 2B **24**
Blagdon. *N Som* 1A **16**
Blagdon Hill. *Som* 2B **24**
Blandford Camp. *Dors* 3A **28**
Blandford Forum. *Dors* 3D **27**
Blandford St Mary. *Dors* 3D **27**
Blashford. *Hants* 3C **29**
Blatchbridge. *Som* 2C **17**
Bleadney. *Som* 2D **15**
Bleadon. *N Som* 1C **15**
Blendworth. *Hants* 2A **32**
Blewbury. *Oxon* 1C **11**
Blindmoor. *Som* 2B **24**
Blissford. *Hants* 2C **29**
Bloxworth. *Dors* 1D **37**
Blunsdon St Andrew. *Swin* 1C **9**
Boarhunt. *Hants* 3D **31**
Bodenham. *Wilts* 1C **29**
Bognor Regis. *W Sus* 3C **33**
Boldre. *Hants* 1A **40**
Bolham Water. *Devn* 2A **24**
Bonchurch. *IOW* 3C **41**
Bonham. *Wilts* 3C **17**
Bonvilston. *V Glam* 2A **4**
Booker. *Buck* 1B **12**
Boorley Green. *Hants* 2C **31**
Borden. *W Sus* 1B **32**
Bordon. *Hants* 3B **22**
Boreham. *Wilts* 2D **17**
Boscombe. *Bour* 1C **39**
Boscombe. *Wilts* 3D **19**
Bosham. *W Sus* 3B **32**
Bothampstead. *W Ber* 2C **11**
Bothenhampton. *Dors* 1D **35**
Botley. *Hants* 2C **31**
Bottlesford. *Wilts* 1C **19**
Bouldnor. *IOW* 2A **40**
Bourne End. *Buck* 1B **12**
Bournemouth. *Bour* 1B **38** & **55**
Bournemouth Airport. *Dors* 1C **39**
Bourne, The. *Surr* 2B **22**
Bourton. *Dors* 3C **17**
Bourton. *N Som* 3C **5**
Bourton. *Oxon* 1D **9**
Bourton. *Wilts* 3B **8**
Boveney. *Buck* 2C **13**
Boveridge. *Dors* 2B **28**
Bovingdon Green. *Buck* 1B **12**
Bovington Camp. *Dors* 2D **37**
Bowcombe. *IOW* 2B **40**
Bowd. *Devn* 2A **34**
Bowden Hill. *Wilts* 3A **8**
Bowdens. *Som* 1D **25**
Bowerchalke. *Wilts* 1B **28**
Bowerhill. *Wilts* 3A **8**
Bower Hinton. *Som* 2D **25**
Bowlhead Green. *Surr* 3C **23**
Bowlish. *Som* 2B **16**
Box. *Wilts* 3D **7**
Boxford. *W Ber* 2B **10**
Boxgrove. *W Sus* 3C **33**
Boys Hill. *Dors* 2B **26**
Boyton. *Wilts* 3A **18**
Bracklesham. *W Sus* 1B **42**
Bracknell. *Brac* 3B **12**
Bradenstoke. *Wilts* 2B **8**
Bradfield. *W Ber* 2D **11**
Bradford Abbas. *Dors* 2A **26**
Bradford Leigh. *Wilts* 3D **7**
Bradford-on-Avon. *Wilts* 3D **7**
Bradford-on-Tone. *Som* 1A **24**
Bradford Peverell. *Dors* 1B **36**
Brading. *IOW* 2D **41**
Bradley. *Glos* 1C **7**
Bradley. *Hants* 2D **21**
Bradley Cross. *Som* 1D **15**
Bradley Green. *Som* 3B **14**
Bradley Stoke. *S Glo* 1B **6**
Bradpole. *Dors* 1D **35**
Braishfield. *Hants* 1A **30**
Brambridge. *Hants* 1B **30**
Bramdean. *Hants* 1D **31**
Bramley. *Hants* 1D **21**
Bramley. *Surr* 2D **23**
Bramley Green. *Hants* 1D **21**
Bramshaw. *Hants* 2D **29**
Bramshill. *Hants* 3A **12**
Bramshott. *Hants* 3B **22**
Branksome. *Pool* 1B **38**
Bransbury. *Hants* 2B **20**
Branscombe. *Devn* 2A **34**
Bransgore. *Hants* 1C **39**
Branstone. *IOW* 2C **41**
Bratton. *Wilts* 1A **18**
Bratton Seymour. *Som* 1B **26**
Bray. *Wind* 2C **13**
Bray Wick. *Wind* 2B **12**
Breach. *W Sus* 3A **32**
Breamore. *Hants* 2C **29**
Brean. *Som* 1B **14**
Bremhill. *Wilts* 2A **8**
Brent Knoll. *Som* 1C **15**
Briantspuddle. *Dors* 1D **37**
Bridge. *Som* 3C **25**
Bridgehampton. *Som* 1A **26**
Bridgemary. *Hants* 3C **31**
Bridgeyate. *S Glo* 2B **6**
Bridgwater. *Som* 3C **15**
Bridport. *Dors* 1D **35**
Brighstone. *IOW* 2B **40**
Brighton Hill. *Hants* 2D **21**
Brightwalton. *W Ber* 2B **10**
Brightwalton Green. *W Ber* 2B **10**
Brightwell-cum-Sotwell. *Oxon* 1C **11**
Brigmerston. *Wilts* 2C **19**
Brimpton. *W Ber* 3C **11**
Brinkworth. *Wilts* 1B **8**
Brinscombe. *Som* 1D **15**
Brislington. *Bris* 2B **6**
Bristol. *Bris* 2A **6** & **56**
Bristol International Airport.
N Som 3A **6**
Britford. *Wilts* 1C **29**
Britwell Salome. *Oxon* 1D **11**
Brixton Deverill. *Wilts* 3D **17**
Broad Blunsdon. *Swin* 1C **9**
Broadbridge. *W Sus* 3B **32**
Broadbridge Heath. *W Sus* 3D **23**
Broad Chalke. *Wilts* 1B **28**
Broadford Bridge. *W Sus* 1D **33**
Broadhembury. *Devn* 3A **24**
Broad Hinton. *Wilts* 2C **9**
Broad Laying. *Hants* 3B **10**
Broadmayne. *Dors* 2C **37**
Broadmere. *Hants* 2D **21**
Broad Oak. *Devn* 1A **34**
Broadoak. *Dors* 1D **35**
Broad Oak. *Dors* 2C **27**
Broadoak. *Hants* 2B **30**
Broadshard. *Som* 2D **25**
Broadstone. *Pool* 1B **38**
Broad Town. *Wilts* 2B **8**
Broadway. *Som* 2C **25**
Broadwey. *Dors* 2B **36**
Broadwindsor. *Dors* 3D **25**
Brockbridge. *Hants* 2D **31**
Brockenhurst. *Hants* 3D **29**
Brockhurst. *Hants* 3C **31**
Brockley. *N Som* 3D **5**
Brokenborough. *Wilts* 1A **8**
Bromham. *Wilts* 3A **8**
Brompton Ralph. *Som* 3A **14**
Brook. *Hants* 2D **29**
(nr. Cadnam)
Brook. *Hants* 1A **30**
(nr. Romsey)
Brook. *IOW* 2A **40**
Brook. *Surr* 2D **23**
(nr. Guildford)
Brook. *Surr* 3C **23**
(nr. Haslemere)
Brooks Green. *W Sus* 1D **33**
Brookwood. *Surr* 1C **23**
Broomer's Corner. *W Sus* 1D **33**
Broomfield. *Som* 3B **14**
Broomhall. *Wind* 3C **13**
Broomhill. *Bris* 2B **6**
Broom Hill. *Dors* 3B **28**
Broughton. *Hants* 3A **20**
Broughton Gifford. *Wilts* 3D **7**
Brown Candover. *Hants* 3C **21**
Brunton. *Wilts* 1D **19**
Bruton. *Som* 3B **16**
Bryanston. *Dors* 3D **27**
Brympton D'Evercy. *Som* 2A **26**
Buckerell. *Devn* 3A **24**
Buckhorn Weston. *Dors* 1C **27**
Buckland Dinham. *Som* 1C **17**
Buckland Newton. *Dors* 3B **26**
Buckland Ripers. *Dors* 2B **36**
Buckland St Mary. *Som* 2B **24**
Bucklebury. *W Ber* 2C **11**
Bucklers Hard. *Hants* 1B **40**
Bucks Green. *W Sus* 3D **23**
Bucks Horn Oak. *Hants* 2B **22**
Budleigh Salterton. *Devn* 2A **34**
Bulford. *Wilts* 2C **19**
Bulford Camp. *Wilts* 2C **19**
Bulkington. *Wilts* 1A **18**
Bull Hill. *Hants* 1A **40**
Burbage. *Wilts* 3D **9**
Burchett's Green. *Wind* 1B **12**
Burcombe. *Wilts* 3B **18**
Burcott. *Som* 2A **16**
Burghclere. *Hants* 3B **10**
Burghfield. *W Ber* 3D **11**
Burghfield Common. *W Ber* 3D **11**
Burghfield Hill. *W Ber* 3D **11**
Buriton. *Hants* 1A **32**
Burleigh. *Brac* 2C **13**
Burlescombe. *Devn* 2A **24**
Burleston. *Dors* 1C **37**
Burley. *Hants* 3D **29**
Burley Street. *Hants* 3D **29**
Burnett. *Bath* 3B **6**
Burnham. *Buck* 1C **13**
Burnham-on-Sea. *Som* 2C **15**
Burntcommon. *Surr* 1D **23**
Burnt Hill. *W Ber* 2C **11**
Burpham. *Surr* 1D **23**
Burpham. *W Sus* 3D **33**
Burridge. *Devn* 3C **25**
Burridge. *Hants* 2C **31**
Burrington. *N Som* 1D **15**
Burrow. *Devn* 2A **34**
Burrowbridge. *Som* 1C **25**
Burrowhill. *Surr* 3C **13**
Bursledon. *Hants* 3B **30**
Burstock. *Dors* 3D **25**
Burtle. *Som* 2D **15**
Burton. *Dors* 1C **39**
(nr. Christchurch)
Burton. *Dors* 1B **36**
(nr. Dorchester)
Burton. *Som* 2A **14**
Burton. *Wilts* 2D **7**
(nr. Chippenham)
Burton. *Wilts* 3D **17**
(nr. Warminster)
Burton Bradstock. *Dors* 2D **35**
Bury. *W Sus* 2D **33**
Bury Hill. *S Glo* 1C **7**
Busbridge. *Surr* 2C **23**
Bushey. *Dors* 2A **38**
Bushton. *Wilts* 2B **8**
Bussex. *Som* 3C **15**
Butcombe. *N Som* 3A **6**
Butleigh. *Som* 3A **16**
Butleigh Wootton. *Som* 3A **16**
Butlocks Heath. *Hants* 3B **30**
Buttermere. *Wilts* 3A **10**
Buttsash. *Hants* 3B **30**
Byfleet. *Surr* 3D **13**
Byworth. *W Sus* 1C **33**

C

Cadley. *Wilts* 1D **19**
(nr. Ludgershall)
Cadley. *Wilts* 3D **9**
(nr. Marlborough)
Cadmore End. *Buck* 1A **12**
Cadnam. *Hants* 2D **29**
Caerau. *Card* 2A **4**
Caerdydd. *Card* 2A **4** & **56**
Caerffili. *Cphy* 1A **4**
Caerleon. *Newp* 1C **5**
Caerllion. *Newp* 1C **5**
Caerphilly. *Cphy* 1A **4**
Caerwent. *Mon* 1D **5**
Calbourne. *IOW* 2B **40**
Calcot Row. *W Ber* 2D **11**
Caldicot. *Mon* 1D **5**
Callow Hill. *Wilts* 1B **8**
Calmore. *Hants* 2A **30**
Calne. *Wilts* 2A **8**
Calshot. *Hants* 3B **30**
Calstone Wellington. *Wilts* 3B **8**
Camberley. *Surr* 3B **12**
Cameley. *Bath* 1B **16**
Camelsdale. *Surr* 3C **23**
Camerton. *Bath* 1B **16**
Canada. *Hants* 2D **29**
Cane End. *Oxon* 2D **11**
Canford Cliffs. *Pool* 2B **38**
Canford Heath. *Pool* 1B **38**
Canford Magna. *Pool* 1B **38**
Cann. *Dors* 1D **27**
Cann Common. *Dors* 1D **27**
Cannington. *Som* 3B **14**
Canton. *Card* 2A **4**
Capel Llanilterne. *Card* 2A **4**
Capton. *Som* 3A **14**
Cardiff. *Card* 2A **4** & **56**
Cardiff International Airport.
V Glam 3A **4**
Carisbrooke. *IOW* 2B **40**
Carlingcott. *Bath* 1B **16**
Carrow Hill. *Mon* 1D **5**
Cartbridge. *Surr* 1D **23**
Carter's Clay. *Hants* 1A **30**
Cas-gwent. *Mon* 1A **6**
Cashmoor. *Dors* 2A **28**
Casnewydd. *Newp* 1C **5**
Castell-y-bwch. *Torf* 1B **4**
Castle. *Som* 2A **16**
Castle Cary. *Som* 3B **16**
Castle Combe. *Wilts* 2D **7**
Castle Green. *Surr* 3C **13**
Castleton. *Newp* 1B **4**
Castletown. *Dors* 3B **36**
Catcott. *Som* 3C **15**
Catherington. *Hants* 2D **31**
Catherston Leweston. *Dors* 1C **35**
Catisfield. *Hants* 3C **31**
Catmore. *W Ber* 1B **10**
Cat's Ash. *Newp* 1C **5**
Catsgore. *Som* 1A **26**
Catteshall. *Surr* 2C **23**
Cattistock. *Dors* 1A **36**
Caversham. *Read* 2A **12**
Caversham Heights. *Read* 2D **11**
Cerne Abbas. *Dors* 3B **26**
Chaddleworth. *W Ber* 2B **10**
Chaffcombe. *Som* 2C **25**
Chalbury. *Dors* 3B **28**
Chalbury Common. *Dors* 3B **28**
Chaldon Herring. *Dors* 2C **37**
Chale. *IOW* 3B **40**
Chale Green. *IOW* 3B **40**
Chalfont Common. *Buck* 1D **13**

Chalfont St Giles—Deanlane End

Chalfont St Giles. *Buck* 1C **13**
Chalfont St Peter. *Buck* 1D **13**
Chalton. *Hants* 2A **32**
Chandler's Ford. *Hants* 1B **30**
Chantry. *Som* 2C **17**
Chapel Allerton. *Som* 1D **15**
Chapel Row. *W Ber* 3C **11**
Chapmanslade. *Wilts* 2D **17**
Chard. *Som* 3C **25**
Chard Junction. *Dors* 3C **25**
Chardstock. *Devn* 3C **25**
Charfield. *S Glo* 1C **7**
Charlcombe. *Bath* 3C **7**
Charlcutt. *Wilts* 2A **8**
Charleshill. *Surr* 2B **22**
Charlestown. *Dors* 3B **36**
Charlton. *Hants* 2A **20**
Charlton. *Oxon* 1B **10**
Charlton. *Som* 1B **16**
(nr. Radstock)
Charlton. *Som* 2B **16**
(nr. Shepton Mallet)
Charlton. *Som* 1B **24**
(nr. Taunton)
Charlton. *W Sus* 2B **32**
Charlton. *Wilts* 1A **8**
(nr. Malmesbury)
Charlton. *Wilts* 1C **19**
(nr. Pewsey)
Charlton. *Wilts* 1C **29**
(nr. Salisbury)
Charlton. *Wilts* 1A **28**
(nr. Shaftesbury)
Charlton Adam. *Som* 1A **26**
Charlton Down. *Dors* 1B **36**
Charlton Horethorne. *Som* 1B **26**
Charlton Mackrell. *Som* 1A **26**
Charlton Marshall. *Dors* 3A **28**
Charlton Musgrove. *Som* 1C **27**
Charlton on the Hill. *Dors* 3D **27**
Charlwood. *Hants* 3D **21**
Charlynch. *Som* 3B **14**
Charminster. *Dors* 1B **36**
Charmouth. *Dors* 1C **35**
Charter Alley. *Hants* 1C **21**
Charterhouse. *Som* 1D **15**
Charvil. *Wok* 2A **12**
Chawton. *Hants* 3A **22**
Cheapside. *Wind* 3C **13**
Checkendon. *Oxon* 1D **11**
Cheddar. *Som* 1D **15**
Cheddon Fitzpaine. *Som* 1B **24**
Chedglow. *Wilts* 1A **8**
Chedington. *Dors* 3D **25**
Chedzoy. *Som* 3C **15**
Chelston. *Som* 1A **24**
Chelvey. *N Som* 3D **5**
Chelwood. *Bath* 3B **6**
Chelworth Lower Green. *Wilts* 1B **8**
Chelworth Upper Green. *Wilts* 1B **8**
Chelynch. *Som* 2B **16**
Chepstow. *Mon* 1A **6**
Cherhill. *Wilts* 2B **8**
Cheriton. *Hants* 1C **31**
Chertsey. *Surr* 3D **13**
Cheselbourne. *Dors* 1C **37**
Chesterblade. *Som* 2B **16**
Chetnole. *Dors* 3B **26**
Chettle. *Dors* 2A **28**
Chew Magna. *Bath* 3A **6**
Chew Stoke. *Bath* 3A **6**
Chewton Keynsham. *Bath* 3B **6**
Chewton Mendip. *Som* 1A **16**
Chichester. *W Sus* 3B **32**
Chickerell. *Dors* 2B **36**
Chicklade. *Wilts* 3A **18**
Chidden. *Hants* 2D **31**
Chiddingfold. *Surr* 3C **23**
Chideock. *Dors* 1D **35**
Chidgley. *Som* 3A **14**
Chidham. *W Sus* 3A **32**
Chieveley. *W Ber* 2B **10**
Chilbolton. *Hants* 2A **20**
Chilcomb. *Hants* 1C **31**
Chilcombe. *Dors* 1A **36**
Chilcompton. *Som* 1B **16**
Child Okeford. *Dors* 2D **27**
Childrey. *Oxon* 1A **10**
Chilfrome. *Dors* 1A **36**
Chilgrove. *W Sus* 2B **32**
Chilhampton. *Wilts* 3B **18**
Chilland. *Hants* 3C **21**
Chillerton. *IOW* 2B **40**
Chillington. *Som* 2C **25**
Chilmark. *Wilts* 3A **18**
Chilthorne Domer. *Som* 2A **26**
Chilton. *Oxon* 1B **10**
Chilton Candover. *Hants* 2C **21**
Chilton Cantelo. *Som* 1A **26**
Chilton Foliat. *Wilts* 2A **10**
Chilton Polden. *Som* 3C **15**
Chilton Trinity. *Som* 3B **14**
Chilworth. *Hants* 2B **30**
Chilworth. *Surr* 2D **23**
Chineham. *Hants* 1D **21**
Chipley. *Som* 1A **24**
Chippenham. *Wilts* 2A **8**
Chipping Sodbury. *S Glo* 1C **7**
Chipstable. *Som* 1A **24**
Chirton. *Wilts* 1B **18**
Chisbridge Cross. *Buck* 1B **12**
Chisbury. *Wilts* 3D **9**
Chiselborough. *Som* 2D **25**
Chiseldon. *Swin* 2C **9**
Chiswell. *Dors* 3B **36**
Chithurst. *W Sus* 1B **32**
Chitterne. *Wilts* 2A **18**
Chittoe. *Wilts* 3A **8**
Chobham. *Surr* 3C **13**
Cholderton. *Wilts* 2D **19**
Cholsey. *Oxon* 1C **11**
Christchurch. *Dors* 1C **39**
Christian Malford. *Wilts* 2A **8**
Christmas Common. *Oxon* 1A **12**
Christon. *N Som* 1C **15**
Church Common. *Hants* 1A **32**
Church Crookham. *Hants* 1B **22**
Church End. *Hants* 1D **21**
Church End. *Wilts* 2B **8**
Church Green. *Devn* 1A **34**
Churchill. *Devn* 3C **25**
Churchill. *N Som* 1D **15**
Churchinford. *Som* 2B **24**
Church Knowle. *Dors* 2A **38**
Church Norton. *W Sus* 1B **42**
Churchstanton. *Som* 2A **24**
Church Village. *Rhon* 1A **4**
Churt. *Surr* 3B **22**
Chute Standen. *Wilts* 1A **20**
Cilfynydd. *Rhon* 1A **4**
Cippenham. *Slo* 1C **13**
Clandown. *Bath* 1B **16**
Clanfield. *Hants* 2D **31**
Clanville. *Hants* 2A **20**
Clanville. *Som* 3B **16**
Clapgate. *Dors* 3B **28**
Clapham. *W Sus* 3D **33**
Clapton. *Som* 3D **25**
(nr. Crewkerne)
Clapton. *Som* 1B **16**
(nr. Radstock)
Clapton-in-Gordano. *N Som* 2D **5**
Clatterford. *IOW* 2B **40**
Clatworthy. *Som* 3A **14**
Claverham. *N Som* 3D **5**
Claverton. *Bath* 3C **7**
Clawdd-coch. *V Glam* 2A **4**
Claygate. *Surr* 3D **13**
Clayhall. *Hants* 1D **41**
Clayhidon. *Devn* 2A **24**
Clay Hill. *Bris* 2B **6**
Clayhill. *Hants* 3A **30**
Cleeve. *N Som* 3D **5**
Cleeve. *Oxon* 1D **11**
Clench Common. *Wilts* 3C **9**
Clevancy. *Wilts* 2B **8**
Clevedon. *N Som* 2D **5**
Cleverton. *Wilts* 1A **8**
Clewer. *Som* 1D **15**
Cliddesden. *Hants* 2D **21**
Clifton. *Bris* 2A **6**
Climping. *W Sus* 3C **33**
Cloford. *Som* 2C **17**
Closworth. *Som* 2A **26**
Clutton. *Bath* 1B **16**
Clyffe Pypard. *Wilts* 2B **8**
Coalpit Heath. *S Glo* 1B **6**
Coat. *Som* 1D **25**
Coate. *Swin* 1C **9**
Coate. *Wilts* 3B **8**
Coates. *W Sus* 2C **33**
Cobham. *Surr* 3D **13**
Cocking. *W Sus* 2B **32**
Cocking Causeway. *W Sus* 2B **32**
Cocklake. *Som* 2D **15**
Cockpole Green. *Wind* 1B **12**
Codford St Mary. *Wilts* 3A **18**
Codford St Peter. *Wilts* 3A **18**
Codmore Hill. *W Sus* 1D **33**
Codrington. *S Glo* 2C **7**
Coedkernew. *Newp* 1B **4**
Cogan. *V Glam* 2A **4**
Colaton Raleigh. *Devn* 2A **34**
Cold Ash. *W Ber* 3C **11**
Cold Ashton. *S Glo* 2C **7**
Colden Common. *Hants* 1B **30**
Cold Harbour. *Dors* 1A **38**
Coldharbour. *Surr* 2D **23**
Coldwaltham. *W Sus* 2D **33**
Cole. *Som* 3B **16**
Coleford. *Som* 2B **16**
Cole Henley. *Hants* 1B **20**
Colehill. *Dors* 3B **28**
Colemore. *Hants* 3A **22**
Colerne. *Wilts* 2D **7**
Coleshill. *Oxon* 1D **9**
Colestocks. *Devn* 3A **24**
Coley. *Bath* 1A **16**
Collingbourne Ducis. *Wilts* 1D **19**
Collingbourne Kingston. *Wilts* 1D **19**
Colliton. *Devn* 3A **24**
Colnbrook. *Slo* 2D **13**
Colworth. *W Sus* 3C **33**
Colyford. *Devn* 1B **34**
Colyton. *Devn* 1B **34**
Combe. *W Ber* 3A **10**
Combe Almer. *Dors* 1A **38**
Combe Common. *Surr* 3C **23**
Combe Down. *Bath* 3C **7**
Combe Florey. *Som* 3A **14**
Combe Hay. *Bath* 1C **17**
Combe Raleigh. *Devn* 3A **24**
Combe St Nicholas. *Som* 2C **25**
Combpyne. *Devn* 1B **34**
Combwich. *Som* 2B **14**
Common Platt. *Wilts* 1C **9**
Common, The. *Wilts* 3D **19**
(nr. Salisbury)
Common, The. *Wilts* 1B **8**
(nr. Swindon)
Compton. *Hants* 1B **30**
Compton. *Surr* 2C **23**
Compton. *W Ber* 1C **11**
Compton. *W Sus* 2A **32**
Compton. *Wilts* 1C **19**
Compton Abbas. *Dors* 2D **27**
Compton Bassett. *Wilts* 2B **8**
Compton Beauchamp. *Oxon* 1D **9**
Compton Bishop. *Som* 1C **15**
Compton Chamberlayne. *Wilts* 1B **28**
Compton Dando. *Bath* 3B **6**
Compton Dundon. *Som* 3D **15**
Compton Greenfield. *S Glo* 1A **6**
Compton Martin. *Bath* 1A **16**
Compton Pauncefoot. *Som* 1B **26**
Compton Valence. *Dors* 1A **36**
Coneyhurst Common. *W Sus* 1D **33**
Conford. *Hants* 3B **22**
Congresbury. *N Som* 3D **5**
Conham. *S Glo* 2B **6**
Conock. *Wilts* 1B **18**
Cookham. *Wind* 1B **12**
Cookham Dean. *Wind* 1B **12**
Cookham Rise. *Wind* 1B **12**
Cookley Green. *Oxon* 1D **11**
Coolham. *W Sus* 1D **33**
Coombe. *Devn* 1A **34**
Coombe. *Glos* 1C **7**
Coombe. *Hants* 1D **31**
Coombe. *Wilts* 1C **19**
Coombe Bissett. *Wilts* 1C **29**
Coombe Keynes. *Dors* 2D **37**
Coombe Street. *Som* 3C **17**
Cootham. *W Sus* 2D **33**
Copythorne. *Hants* 2A **30**
Corfe. *Som* 2B **24**
Corfe Castle. *Dors* 2A **38**
Corfe Mullen. *Dors* 1A **38**
Corhampton. *Hants* 1D **31**
Corscombe. *Dors* 3A **26**
Corsham. *Wilts* 2D **7**
Corsley. *Wilts* 2D **17**
Corsley Heath. *Wilts* 2D **17**
Corston. *Bath* 3B **6**
Corston. *Wilts* 1A **8**
Corton. *Wilts* 2A **18**
Corton Denham. *Som* 1B **26**
Coryates. *Dors* 2B **36**
Coscote. *Oxon* 1C **11**
Cosham. *Port* 3D **31**
Cosmeston. *V Glam* 3A **4**
Cossington. *Som* 2C **15**
Cotford St Luke. *Som* 1A **24**
Cothelstone. *Som* 3A **14**
Cotleigh. *Devn* 3B **24**
Coultershaw Bridge. *W Sus* 2C **33**
Coultings. *Som* 2B **14**
Countess. *Wilts* 2C **19**
Courtway. *Som* 3B **14**
Cove. *Hants* 1B **22**
Covingham. *Swin* 1C **9**
Cowes. *IOW* 1B **40**
Cowley. *G Lon* 1D **13**
Cowplain. *Hants* 2D **31**
Cowslip Green. *N Som* 3D **5**
Cox Green. *Surr* 3D **23**
Coxley. *Som* 2A **16**
Crab Orchard. *Dors* 3B **28**
Craddock. *Devn* 2A **24**
Cranborne. *Dors* 2B **28**
Cranbourne. *Brac* 2C **13**
Cranford. *G Lon* 2D **13**
Cranleigh. *Surr* 3D **23**
Cranmore. *IOW* 1A **40**
Crawley. *Devn* 3B **24**
Crawley. *Hants* 3B **20**
Cray's Pond. *Oxon* 1D **11**
Crazies Hill. *Wok* 1A **12**
Creech. *Dors* 2A **38**
Creech Heathfield. *Som* 1B **24**
Creech St Michael. *Som* 1B **24**
Creekmoor. *Pool* 1A **38**
Creigiau. *Card* 1A **4**
Crendell. *Dors* 2B **28**
Crewkerne. *Som* 3D **25**
Cribbs Causeway. *S Glo* 1A **6**
Crick. *Mon* 1D **5**
Cricket Hill. *Hants* 3B **12**
Cricket Malherbie. *Som* 2C **25**
Cricket St Thomas. *Som* 3C **25**
Crickham. *Som* 2D **15**
Cricklade. *Wilts* 1B **8**
Crimchard. *Som* 3C **25**
Cripplestyle. *Dors* 2B **28**
Crocker End. *Oxon* 1A **12**
Crockerhill. *Hants* 3C **31**
Crockerton. *Wilts* 2D **17**
Croes-y-mwyalch. *Torf* 1C **5**
Croford. *Som* 1A **24**
Crofton. *Wilts* 3D **9**
Cromhall. *S Glo* 1B **6**
Cromhall Common. *S Glo* 1B **6**
Crondall. *Hants* 2A **22**
Crooked Soley. *Wilts* 2A **10**
Crookham. *W Ber* 3C **11**
Crookham Village. *Hants* 1A **22**
Croscombe. *Som* 2A **16**
Cross. *Som* 1D **15**
Crossbush. *W Sus* 3D **33**
Cross Inn. *Rhon* 1A **4**
Crosskeys. *Cphy* 1B **4**
Crossways. *Dors* 2C **37**
Croucheston. *Wilts* 1B **28**
Crouch Hill. *Dors* 2C **27**
Crow. *Hants* 3C **29**
Crowcombe. *Som* 3A **14**
Crowdhill. *Hants* 2B **30**
Crowmarsh Gifford. *Oxon* 1D **11**
Crowthorne. *Brac* 3B **12**
Crudwell. *Wilts* 1A **8**
Crux Easton. *Hants* 1B **20**
Cruxton. *Dors* 1B **36**
Cucklington. *Som* 1C **27**
Cudworth. *Som* 2C **25**
Culm Davy. *Devn* 2A **24**
Culmstock. *Devn* 2A **24**
Cupernham. *Hants* 1A **30**
Curbridge. *Hants* 2C **31**
Curdridge. *Hants* 2C **31**
Curland. *Som* 2B **24**
Curland Common. *Som* 2B **24**
Curridge. *W Ber* 2B **10**
Curry Mallet. *Som* 1C **25**
Curry Rivel. *Som* 1C **25**
Cuttiford's Door. *Som* 2C **25**
Cwmfelinfach. *Cphy* 1A **4**
Cyncoed. *Card* 1A **4**

D

Daggons. *Dors* 2C **29**
Dalwood. *Devn* 3B **24**
Damerham. *Hants* 2C **29**
Daneshill. *Hants* 1D **21**
Datchet. *Wind* 2C **13**
Dauntsey. *Wilts* 1A **8**
Dauntsey Green. *Wilts* 1A **8**
Dauntsey Lock. *Wilts* 1A **8**
Dean. *Dors* 2A **28**
Dean. *Hants* 2C **31**
(nr. Bishop's Waltham)
Dean. *Hants* 3B **20**
(nr. Winchester)
Dean. *Som* 2B **16**
Deane. *Hants* 1C **21**
Deanland. *Dors* 2A **28**
Deanlane End. *W Sus* 2A **32**

Deepcut—Flansham

Deepcut. *Surr* 1C **23**
Denchworth. *Oxon* 1A **10**
Denham. *Buck* 1D **13**
Denham Green. *Buck* 1D **13**
Denmead. *Hants* 2D **31**
Deptford. *Wilts* 3B **18**
Derry Hill. *Wilts* 2A **8**
Devizes. *Wilts* 3B **8**
Dewlish. *Dors* 1C **37**
Dial Green. *W Sus* 1C **33**
Dial Post. *W Sus* 2D **33**
Dibberford. *Dors* 3D **25**
Dibden. *Hants* 3B **30**
Dibden Purlieu. *Hants* 3B **30**
Didcot. *Oxon* 1C **11**
Didling. *W Sus* 2B **32**
Didmarton. *Glos* 1D **7**
Dilton Marsh. *Wilts* 2D **17**
Dimmer. *Som* 3B **16**
Dinas Powys. *V Glam* 2A **4**
Dinder. *Som* 2A **16**
Dinnington. *Som* 2D **25**
Dinton. *Wilts* 3B **18**
Dipley. *Hants* 1A **22**
Dippenhall. *Surr* 2B **22**
Ditchampton. *Wilts* 3B **18**
Ditcheat. *Som* 3B **16**
Ditteridge. *Wilts* 3D **7**
Dodington. *Som* 2A **14**
Dodington. *S Glo* 1C **7**
Dogmersfield. *Hants* 1A **22**
Donhead St Andrew. *Wilts* 1A **28**
Donhead St Mary. *Wilts* 1A **28**
Doniford. *Som* 2A **14**
Donkey Town. *Surr* 3C **13**
Donnington. *W Ber* 3B **10**
Donnington. *W Sus* 3B **32**
Donyatt. *Som* 2C **25**
Dorchester. *Dors* 1B **36**
Dorking. *Surr* 2D **23**
Dorney. *Buck* 2C **13**
Dottery. *Dors* 1D **35**
Doughton. *Glos* 1D **7**
Doulting. *Som* 2B **16**
Dowlands. *Devn* 1B **34**
Dowlesgreen. *Wok* 3B **12**
Dowlish Wake. *Som* 2C **25**
Downend. *IOW* 2C **41**
Downend. *S Glo* 2B **6**
Downend. *W Ber* 2B **10**
Downhead. *Som* 2B **16** (nr. Frome)
Downhead. *Som* 1A **26** (nr. Yeovil)
Downside. *Som* 1B **16** (nr. Chilcompton)
Downside. *Som* 2B **16** (nr. Shepton Mallet)
Downside. *Surr* 1D **23**
Downton. *Hants* 1D **39**
Downton. *Wilts* 1C **29**
Doynton. *S Glo* 2C **7**
Draethen. *Cphy* 1B **4**
Dragons Green. *W Sus* 1D **33**
Draycot Foliat. *Swin* 2C **9**
Draycott. *Som* 1D **15** (nr. Cheddar)
Draycott. *Som* 1A **26** (nr. Yeovil)
Drayton. *Port* 3D **31**
Drayton. *Som* 1D **25**
Drimpton. *Dors* 3D **25**
Droop. *Dors* 3C **27**
Drope. *V Glam* 2A **4**
Droxford. *Hants* 2D **31**
Duck Street. *Hants* 2A **20**
Dulcote. *Som* 2A **16**
Dulford. *Devn* 3A **24**
Dummer. *Hants* 2C **21**
Dumpford. *W Sus* 1B **32**
Dunball. *Som* 2C **15**
Dunbridge. *Hants* 1A **30**
Duncton. *W Sus* 2C **33**
Dundon. *Som* 3D **15**
Dundridge. *Hants* 2C **31**
Dundry. *N Som* 3A **6**
Dunge. *Wilts* 1D **17**
Dunkerton. *Bath* 1C **17**
Dunkeswell. *Devn* 3A **24**
Dunkirk. *S Glo* 1C **7**
Dunkirk. *Wilts* 3A **8**
Dunley. *Hants* 1B **20**
Dunsden Green. *Oxon* 2A **12**
Dunsfold. *Surr* 3D **23**
Duntish. *Dors* 3B **26**
Durleigh. *Som* 3B **14**
Durley. *Hants* 2C **31**
Durley. *Wilts* 3D **9**
Durley Street. *Hants* 2C **31**
Durns Town. *Hants* 1D **39**
Durrants. *Hants* 2A **32**
Durrington. *W Sus* 3D **33**
Durrington. *Wilts* 2C **19**
Durston. *Som* 1B **24**
Durweston. *Dors* 3D **27**
Dyffryn. *V Glam* 2A **4**
Dyrham. *S Glo* 2C **7**

E

Earley. *Wok* 2A **12**
Earnley. *W Sus* 1B **42**
Eartham. *W Sus* 3C **33**
Earthcott Green. *S Glo* 1B **6**
Easebourne. *W Sus* 1B **32**
Eashing. *Surr* 2C **23**
East Anton. *Hants* 2A **20**
East Ashling. *W Sus* 3B **32**
East Aston. *Hants* 2B **20**
East Beach. *W Sus* 1B **42**
East Bedfont. *G Lon* 2D **13**
East Bloxworth. *Dors* 1D **37**
East Boldre. *Hants* 3A **30**
East Brent. *Som* 1C **15**
East Budleigh. *Devn* 2A **34**
East Burnham. *Buck* 1C **13**
East Burton. *Dors* 2D **37**
Eastbury. *Herts* 1D **13**
Eastbury. *W Ber* 2A **10**
East Chaldon. *Dors* 2C **37**
East Challow. *Oxon* 1A **10**
East Chelborough. *Dors* 3A **26**
East Chinnock. *Som* 2D **25**
East Chisenbury. *Wilts* 1C **19**
East Clandon. *Surr* 1D **23**
East Clevedon. *N Som* 2D **5**
East Coker. *Som* 2A **26**
East Combe. *Som* 3A **14**
East Compton. *Som* 2B **16**
Eastcote. *G Lon* 1D **13**
Eastcott. *Wilts* 1B **18**
East Coulston. *Wilts* 1A **18**
Eastcourt. *Wilts* 3D **9** (nr. Pewsey)
Eastcourt. *Wilts* 1A **8** (nr. Tetbury)
East Cowes. *IOW* 1C **41**
East Cranmore. *Som* 2B **16**
East Creech. *Dors* 2A **38**
East Dean. *Hants* 1D **29**
East Dean. *W Sus* 2C **33**
East Dundry. *N Som* 3A **6**
East End. *Dors* 1A **38**
East End. *Hants* 1A **40** (nr. Lymington)
East End. *Hants* 3B **10** (nr. Newbury)
East End. *N Som* 2D **5**
East End. *Som* 1A **16**
Easter Compton. *S Glo* 1A **6**
Eastergate. *W Sus* 3C **33**
Easterton. *Wilts* 1B **18**
Eastertown. *Som* 1C **15**
East Everleigh. *Wilts* 1D **19**
East Garston. *W Ber* 2A **10**
East Ginge. *Oxon* 1B **10**
East Grafton. *Wilts* 3D **9**
East Grimstead. *Wilts* 1D **29**
East Hagbourne. *Oxon* 1C **11**
Easthampstead. *Brac* 3B **12**
East Hanney. *Oxon* 1B **10**
East Harnham. *Wilts* 1C **29**
East Harptree. *Bath* 1A **16**
East Harting. *W Sus* 2B **32**
East Hatch. *Wilts* 1A **28**
Eastheath. *Wok* 3B **12**
East Hendred. *Oxon* 1B **10**
East Holme. *Dors* 2D **37**
East Horrington. *Som* 2A **16**
East Horsley. *Surr* 1D **23**
East Howe. *Bour* 1B **38**
East Huntspill. *Som* 2C **15**
East Ilsley. *W Ber* 1B **10**
East Kennett. *Wilts* 3C **9**
East Knighton. *Dors* 2D **37**
East Knoyle. *Wilts* 3D **17**
East Lambrook. *Som* 2D **25**
East Lavant. *W Sus* 3B **32**
East Lavington. *W Sus* 2C **33**
Eastleigh. *Hants* 2B **30**
East Liss. *Hants* 1A **32**
East Lockinge. *Oxon* 1B **10**
East Lulworth. *Dors* 2D **37**
East Lydford. *Som* 3A **16**
East Lyng. *Som* 1C **25**
East Marden. *W Sus* 2B **32**
East Meon. *Hants* 1D **31**
East Molesey. *Surr* 3D **13**
East Morden. *Dors* 1A **38**
Eastney. *Port* 1D **41**
East Nynehead. *Som* 1A **24**
East Oakley. *Hants* 1C **21**
Easton. *Dors* 3B **36**
Easton. *Hants* 3C **21**
Easton. *Som* 2A **16**
Easton. *Wilts* 2D **7**
Easton Grey. *Wilts* 1D **7**
Easton-in-Gordano. *N Som* 2A **6**
Easton Royal. *Wilts* 3D **9**
East Orchard. *Dors* 2D **27**
East Pennard. *Som* 3A **16**
East Preston. *W Sus* 3D **33**
East Quantoxhead. *Som* 2A **14**
East Shefford. *W Ber* 2A **10**
East Stoke. *Dors* 2D **37**
East Stoke. *Som* 2D **25**
East Stour. *Dors* 1D **27**
East Stratton. *Hants* 2C **21**
East Tisted. *Hants* 3A **22**
East Tytherley. *Hants* 1D **29**
East Tytherton. *Wilts* 2A **8**
East Wellow. *Hants* 1A **30**
East Winterslow. *Wilts* 3D **19**
East Wittering. *W Sus* 1A **42**
East Woodhay. *Hants* 3B **10**
East Woodlands. *Som* 2C **17**
East Worldham. *Hants* 3A **22**
Ebbesbourne Wake. *Wilts* 1A **28**
Ebblake. *Dors* 3C **29**
Ecchinswell. *Hants* 1C **21**
Eddington. *W Ber* 3A **10**
Edgarley. *Som* 3A **16**
Edington. *Som* 3C **15**
Edington. *Wilts* 1A **18**
Edingworth. *Som* 1C **15**
Edithmead. *Som* 2C **15**
Edmondsham. *Dors* 2B **28**
Efail Isaf. *Rhon* 1A **4**
Effingham. *Surr* 1D **23**
Effingham Common. *Surr* 1D **23**
Egbury. *Hants* 1B **20**
Egham. *Surr* 2D **13**
Egham Hythe. *Surr* 2D **13**
Egypt. *Buck* 1C **13**
Egypt. *Hants* 2B **20**
Elberton. *S Glo* 1B **6**
Elbridge. *W Sus* 3C **33**
Elcombe. *Swin* 1C **9**
Elcot. *W Ber* 3A **10**
Eling. *Hants* 2A **30**
Eling. *W Ber* 2C **11**
Ellen's Green. *Surr* 3D **23**
Ellingham. *Hants* 3C **29**
Ellisfield. *Hants* 2D **21**
Elmfield. *IOW* 1C **41**
Elm Hill. *Dors* 1D **27**
Elstead. *Surr* 2C **23**
Elsted. *W Sus* 2B **32**
Elsted Marsh. *W Sus* 1B **32**
Elston. *Wilts* 2B **18**
Elvetham Heath. *Hants* 1A **22**
Elworth. *Dors* 2A **36**
Elworthy. *Som* 3A **14**
Ely. *Card* 2A **4**
Emborough. *Som* 1B **16**
Emery Down. *Hants* 3D **29**
Emmbrook. *Wok* 3A **12**
Emmer Green. *Read* 2A **12**
Empshott. *Hants* 3A **22**
Emsworth. *Hants* 3A **32**
Enborne. *W Ber* 3B **10**
Enborne Row. *W Ber* 3B **10**
Enford. *Wilts* 1C **19**
Engine Common. *S Glo* 1B **6**
Englefield. *W Ber* 2D **11**
Englefield Green. *Surr* 2C **13**
Englishcombe. *Bath* 3C **7**
Enham Alamein. *Hants* 2A **20**
Enmore. *Som* 3B **14**
Ensbury. *Bour* 1B **38**
Erlestoke. *Wilts* 1A **18**
Esher. *Surr* 3D **13**
Etchilhampton. *Wilts* 3B **8**
Eton. *Wind* 2C **13**
Eton Wick. *Wind* 2C **13**
Even Swindon. *Swin* 1C **9**
Evercreech. *Som* 3B **16**
Everleigh. *Wilts* 1D **19**
Evershot. *Dors* 3A **26**
Eversley. *Hants* 3A **12**
Eversley Centre. *Hants* 3A **12**
Eversley Cross. *Hants* 3A **12**
Everton. *Hants* 1D **39**
Ewelme. *Oxon* 1D **11**
Ewhurst. *Surr* 2D **23**
Ewhurst Green. *Surr* 3D **23**
Ewshot. *Hants* 1B **22**
Exbury. *Hants* 3B **30**
Exlade Street. *Oxon* 1D **11**
Exton. *Hants* 1D **31**

F

Faccombe. *Hants* 1A **20**
Failand. *N Som* 2A **6**
Fairlands. *Surr* 1C **23**
Fairmile. *Devn* 1A **34**
Fairmile. *Surr* 3D **13**
Fair Oak. *Hants* 2B **30** (nr. Eastleigh)
Fair Oak. *Hants* 3C **11** (nr. Kingsclere)
Fair Oak Green. *Hants* 3D **11**
Fairwater. *Card* 2A **4**
Falfield. *S Glo* 1B **6**
Fareham. *Hants* 3C **31**
Farleigh. *N Som* 3D **5**
Farleigh Hungerford. *Som* 1D **17**
Farleigh Wallop. *Hants* 2D **21**
Farleigh Wick. *Wilts* 3D **7**
Farley. *N Som* 2D **5**
Farley. *Wilts* 1D **29**
Farley Green. *Surr* 2D **23**
Farley Hill. *Wok* 3A **12**
Farlington. *Port* 3D **31**
Farmborough. *Bath* 3B **6**
Farnborough. *Hants* 1B **22**
Farnborough. *W Ber* 1B **10**
Farnborough Airport. *Surr* 1B **22**
Farncombe. *Surr* 2C **23**
Farnham. *Dors* 2A **28**
Farnham. *Surr* 2B **22**
Farnham Common. *Buck* 1C **13**
Farnham Royal. *Buck* 1C **13**
Farrington. *Dors* 2D **27**
Farrington Gurney. *Bath* 1B **16**
Farway. *Devn* 1A **34**
Faulkland. *Som* 1C **17**
Fawley. *Buck* 1A **12**
Fawley. *Hants* 3B **30**
Fawley. *W Ber* 1A **10**
Felpham. *W Sus* 3C **33**
Feltham. *G Lon* 2D **13**
Felthamhill. *Surr* 2D **13**
Felton. *N Som* 3A **6**
Feniton. *Devn* 1A **34**
Fenny Bridges. *Devn* 1A **34**
Ferndown. *Dors* 3B **28**
Fernham. *Oxon* 1D **9**
Fernhurst. *W Sus* 1B **32**
Ferring. *W Sus* 3D **33**
Fetcham. *Surr* 1D **23**
Ffont-y-gari. *V Glam* 3A **4**
Ffwl-y-mwn. *V Glam* 3A **4**
Fiddington. *Som* 2B **14**
Fiddleford. *Dors* 2D **27**
Fifehead Magdalen. *Dors* 1C **27**
Fifehead Neville. *Dors* 2C **27**
Fifehead St Quintin. *Dors* 2C **27**
Fifield. *Wilts* 1C **19**
Fifield. *Wind* 2C **13**
Fifield Bavant. *Wilts* 1B **28**
Figheldean. *Wilts* 2C **19**
Filford. *Dors* 1D **35**
Filton. *S Glo* 2B **6**
Finchampstead. *Wok* 3A **12**
Finchdean. *Hants* 2A **32**
Findon. *W Sus* 3D **33**
Findon Valley. *W Sus* 3D **33**
Fingest. *Buck* 1A **12**
Firsdown. *Wilts* 3D **19**
Fishbourne. *IOW* 1C **41**
Fishbourne. *W Sus* 3B **32**
Fisher's Pond. *Hants* 1B **30**
Fisherstreet. *W Sus* 3C **23**
Fisherton de la Mere. *Wilts* 3A **18**
Fishpond Bottom. *Dors* 1C **35**
Fishponds. *Bris* 2B **6**
Fittleton. *Wilts* 2C **19**
Fittleworth. *W Sus* 2D **33**
Fitzhead. *Som* 1A **24**
Five Bells. *Som* 2A **14**
Fivehead. *Som* 1C **25**
Five Oaks. *W Sus* 1D **33**
Flackwell Heath. *Buck* 1B **12**
Flansham. *W Sus* 3C **33**

Flax Bourton—Hill Head

Flax Bourton. *N Som* 3A 6
Flaxpool. *Som* 3A 14
Fleet. *Dors* 2B 36
Fleet. *Hants* 1B 22
(nr. Farnborough)
Fleet. *Hants* 3A 32
(nr. South Hayling)
Flexford. *Surr* 1C 23
Fluxton. *Devn* 1A 34
Foddington. *Som* 1A 26
Folke. *Dors* 2B 26
Folly, The. *W Ber* 3B 10
Fonmon. *V Glam* 3A 4
Fonthill Bishop. *Wilts* 3A 18
Fonthill Gifford. *Wilts* 3A 18
Fontmell Magna. *Dors* 2D 27
Fontwell. *W Sus* 3C 33
Font-y-gary. *V Glam* 3A 4
Ford. *Som* 1A 16
(nr. Wells)
Ford. *Som* 1A 24
(nr. Wiveliscombe)
Ford. *W Sus* 3D 33
Ford. *Wilts* 2D 7
(nr. Chippenham)
Ford. *Wilts* 3C 19
(nr. Salisbury)
Fordingbridge. *Hants* 2C 29
Ford Street. *Som* 2A 24
Forest Green. *Surr* 2D 23
Forestside. *W Sus* 2A 32
Forston. *Dors* 1B 36
Forton. *Hants* 2B 20
Forton. *Som* 3C 25
Fortuneswell. *Dors* 3B 36
Forty Green. *Buck* 1C 13
Fosbury. *Wilts* 1A 20
Four Forks. *Som* 3B 14
Four Marks. *Hants* 3D 21
Fovant. *Wilts* 1B 28
Fox Corner. *Surr* 1C 23
Foxcote. *Som* 1C 17
Foxham. *Wilts* 2A 8
Fox Lane. *Hants* 1B 22
Foxley. *Wilts* 1D 7
Frampton. *Dors* 1B 36
Frampton Cotterell. *S Glo* 1B 6
Fratton. *Port* 3D 31
Freefolk Priors. *Hants* 2B 20
Frensham. *Surr* 2B 22
Freshford. *Bath* 3C 7
Freshwater. *IOW* 2A 40
Freshwater Bay. *IOW* 2A 40
Friar Waddon. *Dors* 2B 36
Friday Street. *Surr* 2D 23
Frieth. *Buck* 1A 12
Frilsham. *W Ber* 2C 11
Frimley. *Surr* 1B 22
Frimley Green. *Surr* 1B 22
Fritham. *Hants* 2D 29
Frogham. *Hants* 2C 29
Frogmore. *Hants* 3B 12
Frome. *Som* 2C 17
Fromefield. *Som* 2C 17
Frome St Quintin. *Dors* 3A 26
Froxfield. *Wilts* 3D 9
Froxfield Green. *Hants* 1A 32
Fryern Hill. *Hants* 1B 30
Fugglestone St Peter. *Wilts* 3C 19
Fulflood. *Hants* 3B 20
Fulford. *Som* 1B 24
Fullerton. *Hants* 3A 20
Fulmer. *Buck* 1C 13
Fulwood. *Som* 2B 24
Funtington. *W Sus* 3B 32
Funtley. *Hants* 3C 31
Furley. *Devn* 3B 24
Furzebrook. *Dors* 2A 38
Furzehill. *Dors* 3B 28
Furzeley Corner. *Hants* 2D 31
Furzey Lodge. *Hants* 3A 30
Furzley. *Hants* 2D 29
Fyfield. *Hants* 2D 19
Fyfield. *Wilts* 3C 9
Fyning. *W Sus* 1B 32

G

Galhampton. *Som* 1B 26
Gallowstree Common. *Oxon* 1D 11
Galmington. *Som* 1B 24
Galton. *Dors* 2C 37
Gardeners Green. *Wok* 3B 12
Gare Hill. *Som* 2C 17
Garsdon. *Wilts* 1A 8
Gasper. *Wilts* 3C 17
Gastard. *Wilts* 3D 7
Gatcombe. *IOW* 2B 40
Gaunt's Common. *Dors* 3B 28
Gaunt's Earthcott. *S Glo* 1B 6
Gay Street. *W Sus* 1D 33
George Green. *Buck* 1C 13
Gerrards Cross. *Buck* 1C 13
Giddeahall. *Wilts* 2D 7
Gillingham. *Dors* 1D 27
Gittisham. *Devn* 1A 34
Glanvilles Wootton. *Dors* 3B 26
Glastonbury. *Som* 3D 15
Glyncoch. *Rhon* 1A 4
Glyntaff. *Rhon* 1A 4
Goatacre. *Wilts* 2B 8
Goathill. *Dors* 2B 26
Goathurst. *Som* 3B 14
Godalming. *Surr* 2C 23
Godford Cross. *Devn* 3A 24
Godmanstone. *Dors* 1B 36
Godshill. *Hants* 2C 29
Godshill. *IOW* 2C 41
Goldcliff. *Newp* 1C 5
Golden Pot. *Hants* 2A 22
Gomeldon. *Wilts* 3C 19
Gomshall. *Surr* 2D 23
Goodworth Clatford. *Hants* 2A 20
Goose Green. *S Glo* 1C 7
Goosey. *Oxon* 1A 10
Gores. *Wilts* 1C 19
Goring. *Oxon* 1D 11
Goring-by-Sea. *W Sus* 3D 33
Goring Heath. *Oxon* 2D 11
Gosport. *Hants* 3D 31
Graffham. *W Sus* 2C 33
Grafham. *Surr* 2D 23
Grangetown. *Card* 2A 4
Grateley. *Hants* 2D 19
Grayshott. *Hants* 3B 22
Grayswood. *Surr* 3C 23
Grazeley. *Wok* 3D 11
Great Bedwyn. *Wilts* 3D 9
Great Bookham. *Surr* 1D 23
Great Chalfield. *Wilts* 3D 7
Great Cheverell. *Wilts* 1A 18
Great Coxwell. *Oxon* 1D 9
Great Durnford. *Wilts* 3C 19
Great Elm. *Som* 2C 17
Greatham. *Hants* 3A 22
Greatham. *W Sus* 2D 33
Great Hinton. *Wilts* 1A 18
Great Shefford. *W Ber* 2A 10
Great Shoddesden. *Hants* 2D 19
Great Somerford. *Wilts* 1A 8
Great Thorness. *IOW* 1B 40
Great Wishford. *Wilts* 3B 18
Greendown. *Som* 1A 16
Greenfield. *Oxon* 1A 12
Greenford. *G Lon* 1D 13
Greenham. *Dors* 3D 25
Greenham. *Som* 1A 24
Greenham. *W Ber* 3B 10
Green Ore. *Som* 1A 16
Green, The. *Wilts* 3D 17
Greenway. *V Glam* 2A 4
Greinton. *Som* 3D 15
Greylake. *Som* 3C 15
Greywell. *Hants* 1A 22
Griggs Green. *Hants* 3B 22
Grimstone. *Dors* 1B 36
Grittenham. *Wilts* 1B 8
Grittleton. *Wilts* 2D 7
Groes-faen. *Rhon* 1A 4
Groes-wen. *Cphy* 1A 4
Grove. *Dors* 3C 37
Grove. *Oxon* 1A 10
Guildford. *Surr* 2C 23 & 57
Gundleton. *Hants* 3D 21
Gunville. *IOW* 2B 40
Gurnard. *IOW* 1B 40
Gurney Slade. *Som* 2B 16
Gussage All Saints. *Dors* 2B 28
Gussage St Andrew. *Dors* 2A 28
Gussage St Michael. *Dors* 2A 28
Guy's Marsh. *Dors* 1D 27
Gwaelod-y-garth. *Card* 1A 4
Gwaun-y-bara. *Cphy* 1A 4

H

Habin. *W Sus* 1B 32
Hale. *Hants* 2C 29
Hale. *Surr* 2B 22
Halfway. *W Ber* 3B 10
Hallatrow. *Bath* 1B 16
Hallen. *S Glo* 1A 6
Halnaker. *W Sus* 3C 33
Halse. *Som* 1A 24
Halstock. *Dors* 3A 26
Halsway. *Som* 3A 14
Ham. *Devn* 3B 24
Ham. *Som* 2B 24
(nr. Ilminster)
Ham. *Som* 1B 24
(nr. Taunton)
Ham. *Som* 1A 24
(nr. Wellington)
Ham. *Wilts* 3A 10
Hambleden. *Buck* 1A 12
Hambledon. *Hants* 2D 31
Hambledon. *Surr* 3C 23
Hamble-le-Rice. *Hants* 3B 30
Hambridge. *Som* 1C 25
Hambrook. *S Glo* 2B 6
Hambrook. *W Sus* 3A 32
Ham Common. *Dors* 1D 27
Ham Green. *N Som* 2A 6
Hammer. *W Sus* 3B 22
Hammoon. *Dors* 2D 27
Hamp. *Som* 3C 15
Hampreston. *Dors* 1B 38
Hampstead Norreys. *W Ber* 2C 11
Hampton. *Devn* 1B 34
Hampton. *G Lon* 2D 13
Hampton. *Swin* 1C 9
Hamptworth. *Wilts* 2D 29
Hamstead. *IOW* 1B 40
Hamstead Marshall. *W Ber* 3B 10
Ham Street. *Som* 3A 16
Hamworthy. *Pool* 1A 38
Hand and Pen. *Devn* 1A 34
Hanford. *Dors* 2D 27
Hangersley. *Hants* 3C 29
Hanging Langford. *Wilts* 3B 18
Hangleton. *W Sus* 3D 33
Hanham. *S Glo* 2B 6
Hanham Green. *S Glo* 2B 6
Hankerton. *Wilts* 1A 8
Hannington. *Hants* 1C 21
Hannington. *Swin* 1C 9
Hanwell. *G Lon* 1D 13
Hanworth. *G Lon* 2D 13
Harbridge. *Hants* 2C 29
Harcombe. *Devn* 1A 34
Harcombe Bottom. *Devn* 1C 35
Hardenhuish. *Wilts* 2A 8
Hardham. *W Sus* 2D 33
Hardington. *Som* 1C 17
Hardington Mandeville. *Som* 2A 26
Hardington Marsh. *Som* 3A 26
Hardington Moor. *Som* 2A 26
Hardley. *Hants* 3B 30
Hardway. *Hants* 3D 31
Hardway. *Som* 3C 17
Hare. *Som* 2B 24
Harefield. *G Lon* 1D 13
Hare Hatch. *Wok* 2B 12
Harlington. *G Lon* 2D 13
Harman's Cross. *Dors* 2A 38
Harmondsworth. *G Lon* 2D 13
Harpford. *Devn* 1A 34
Harpsden. *Oxon* 1A 12
Harry Stoke. *S Glo* 2B 6
Hartfordbridge. *Hants* 1A 22
Hartley Mauditt. *Hants* 3A 22
Hartley Wespall. *Hants* 1D 21
Hartley Wintney. *Hants* 1A 22
Hartswell. *Som* 1A 24
Harwell. *Oxon* 1B 10
Hascombe. *Surr* 3C 23
Haselbury Plucknett. *Som* 2D 25
Haslemere. *Surr* 3C 23
Haste Hill. *Surr* 3C 23
Hatch Beauchamp. *Som* 1C 25
Hatch End. *G Lon* 1D 13
Hatch Green. *Som* 2C 25
Hatch Warren. *Hants* 2D 21
Hatherden. *Hants* 1A 20
Hattingley. *Hants* 3D 21
Hatton. *G Lon* 2D 13
Havant. *Hants* 3A 32
Havenstreet. *IOW* 1C 41
Haven, The. *W Sus* 3D 23
Havyatt. *Som* 3A 16
Hawkchurch. *Devn* 3C 25
Hawkeridge. *Wilts* 1D 17
Hawkerland. *Devn* 2A 34
Hawkesbury. *S Glo* 1C 7
Hawkesbury Upton. *S Glo* 1C 7
Hawkley. *Hants* 1A 32
Hawley. *Hants* 1B 22
Hawthorn Hill. *Brac* 2B 12
Haybridge. *Som* 2A 16
Haydon. *Bath* 1B 16
Haydon. *Dors* 2B 26
Haydon. *Som* 1B 24
Haydon Wick. *Swin* 1C 9
Hayes. *G Lon* 1D 13
Haylands. *IOW* 1C 41
Hayling Island. *Hants* 1A 42
Hazelbury Bryan. *Dors* 3C 27
Hazeley. *Hants* 1A 22
Headbourne Worthy. *Hants* 3B 20
Headley. *Hants* 3B 22
(nr. Haslemere)
Headley. *Hants* 3C 11
(nr. Kingsclere)
Headley Down. *Hants* 3B 22
Headley Park. *Bris* 3A 6
Heath Common. *W Sus* 2D 33
Heath End. *Hants* 3C 11
Heathfield. *Som* 3A 14
(nr. Lydeard St Lawrence)
Heathfield. *Som* 1A 24
(nr. Norton Fitzwarren)
Heath House. *Som* 2D 15
Heathrow (London) Airport.
G Lon 2D 13
Heathstock. *Devn* 3B 24
Heckfield. *Hants* 3A 12
Heddington. *Wilts* 3A 8
Hedge End. *Hants* 2B 30
Hedgerley. *Buck* 1C 13
Hedging. *Som* 1C 25
Helland. *Som* 1C 25
Hemington. *Som* 1C 17
Hemsworth. *Dors* 3A 28
Hemyock. *Devn* 2A 24
Henbury. *Bris* 2A 6
Henfield. *S Glo* 2B 6
Henlade. *Som* 1B 24
Henley. *Dors* 3B 26
Henley. *Som* 3D 15
Henley. *W Sus* 1B 32
Henley-on-Thames. *Oxon* 1A 12
Hensting. *Hants* 1B 30
Henstridge. *Som* 2C 27
Henstridge Ash. *Som* 1C 27
Henstridge Bowden. *Som* 1B 26
Henstridge Marsh. *Som* 1C 27
Henton. *Som* 2D 15
Hermitage. *Dors* 3B 26
Hermitage. *W Ber* 2C 11
Hermitage. *W Sus* 3A 32
Herriard. *Hants* 2D 21
Hersham. *Surr* 3D 13
Herston. *Dors* 3B 38
Heston. *G Lon* 2D 13
Hewish. *N Som* 3C 5
Hewish. *Som* 3D 25
Hewood. *Dors* 3C 25
Heyshott. *W Sus* 2B 32
Heytesbury. *Wilts* 2A 18
Heywood. *Wilts* 1D 17
Highbridge. *Som* 2C 15
Highbury. *Som* 2B 16
Highclere. *Hants* 3B 10
Highcliffe. *Dors* 1D 39
High Cross. *Hants* 1A 32
Higher Alham. *Som* 2B 16
Higher Ansty. *Dors* 3C 27
Higher Bockhampton. *Dors* 1C 37
Higher Cheriton. *Devn* 3A 24
Higher Halstock Leigh. *Dors* 3A 26
Higher Kingcombe. *Dors* 1A 36
Higher Melcombe. *Dors* 3C 27
Higher Tale. *Devn* 3A 24
Higher Vexford. *Som* 3A 14
Higher Whatcombe. *Dors* 3D 27
Higher Wraxall. *Dors* 3A 26
High Ham. *Som* 3D 15
Highleigh. *W Sus* 1B 42
High Littleton. *Bath* 1B 16
Highmoor. *Oxon* 1A 12
Highmoor Hill. *Mon* 1D 5
High Salvington. *W Sus* 3D 33
Highstreet Green. *Surr* 3C 23
Highworth. *Swin* 1D 9
High Wycombe. *Buck* 1B 12
Hilcott. *Wilts* 1C 19
Hilfield. *Dors* 3B 26
Hillbourne. *Pool* 1B 38
Hill Brow. *Hants* 1A 32
Hillbutts. *Dors* 3A 28
Hillcommon. *Som* 1A 24
Hill Deverill. *Wilts* 2D 17
Hillesley. *Glos* 1C 7
Hillfarrance. *Som* 1A 24
Hillgreen. *W Ber* 2B 10
Hill Head. *Hants* 3C 31

Southern England Regional Atlas 47

New Denham—Poulner

New Denham. *Buck* 1D 13
Newell Green. *Brac* 2B 12
Newfound. *Hants* 1C 21
New Haw. *Surr* 3D 13
New Mill. *Wilts* 3C 9
New Milton. *Hants* 1D 39
Newnham. *Hants* 1A 22
Newport. *IOW* 2C 41
Newport. *Newp* 1C 5
Newport. *Som* 1C 25
Newpound Common. *W Sus* 1D 33
New Swanage. *Dors* 2B 38
Newton. *Dors* 2C 27
Newton. *Som* 3A 14
Newton. *Wilts* 1D 29
Newton Green. *Mon* 1A 6
Newton Poppleford. *Devn* 2A 34
Newton St Loe. *Bath* 3C 7
Newton Stacey. *Hants* 2B 20
Newton Toney. *Wilts* 2D 19
Newton Tony. *Wilts* 2D 19
Newton Valence. *Hants* 3A 22
Newtown. *Dors* 3D 25
(nr. Beaminster)
New Town. *Dors* 2A 28
(nr. Sixpenny Handley)
Newtown. *Hants* 2C 31
(nr. Bishop's Waltham)
Newtown. *Hants* 2D 29
(nr. Lyndhurst)
Newtown. *Hants* 3B 10
(nr. Newbury)
Newtown. *Hants* 1A 30
(nr. Romsey)
Newtown. *Hants* 3B 30
(nr. Warsash)
Newtown. *Hants* 2D 31
(nr. Wickham)
Newtown. *IOW* 1B 40
Newtown. *Pool* 1B 38
Newtown. *Som* 2B 24
Newtown. *Wilts* 1A 28
Newyears Green. *G Lon* 1D 13
Nicholashayne. *Devn* 2A 24
Nimmer. *Som* 2C 25
Nine Elms. *Swin* 1C 9
Ningwood. *IOW* 2B 40
Niton. *IOW* 3C 41
Nomansland. *Wilts* 2D 29
Norleywood. *Hants* 1A 40
Normandy. *Surr* 1C 23
Norman's Green. *Devn* 3A 24
Norrington Common. *Wilts* 3D 7
Northam. *Sotn* 2B 30
North Ascot. *Brac* 3C 13
Northay. *Som* 2B 24
North Baddesley. *Hants* 1A 30
North Barrow. *Som* 1B 26
North Bersted. *W Sus* 3C 33
North Boarhunt. *Hants* 2D 31
North Bockhampton. *Dors* 1C 39
Northbourne. *Oxon* 1C 11
North Bowood. *Dors* 1D 35
North Bradley. *Wilts* 1D 17
North Brewham. *Som* 3C 17
North Cadbury. *Som* 1B 26
Northchapel. *W Sus* 1C 33
North Charford. *Hants* 2C 29
North Cheriton. *Som* 1B 26
North Chideock. *Dors* 1D 35
North Coker. *Som* 2A 26
Northcott. *Devn* 2A 24
North Curry. *Som* 1C 25
Northend. *Buck* 1A 12
North End. *Hants* 3B 10
North End. *N Som* 3D 5
North End. *Port* 3D 31
North End. *W Sus* 3D 33
Northfield. *Som* 3B 14
North Gorley. *Hants* 2C 29
North Hayling. *Hants* 3A 32
North Heath. *W Sus* 1D 33
Northington. *Hants* 3C 21
Northleigh. *Devn* 1A 34
North Marden. *W Sus* 2B 32
Northmoor Green. *Som* 3C 15
North Moreton. *Oxon* 1C 11
North Mundham. *W Sus* 3B 32
North Newnton. *Wilts* 1C 19
North Newton. *Som* 3B 14
Northney. *Hants* 3A 32
North Oakley. *Hants* 1C 21
Northolt. *G Lon* 1D 13
Northover. *Som* 3D 15
(nr. Glastonbury)
Northover. *Som* 1A 26
(nr. Yeovil)
North Perrott. *Som* 3D 25
North Petherton. *Som* 3B 14
North Poorton. *Dors* 1A 36
Northport. *Dors* 2A 38
North Stoke. *Bath* 3C 7
North Stoke. *Oxon* 1D 11
North Stoke. *W Sus* 2D 33
North Street. *Hants* 3D 21
North Street. *W Ber* 2D 11
North Waltham. *Hants* 2C 21
North Warnborough. *Hants* 1A 22
North Weston. *N Som* 2D 5
North Wick. *Bath* 3A 6
Northwick. *Som* 2C 15
Northwick. *S Glo* 1A 6
North Widcombe. *Bath* 1A 16
Northwood. *G Lon* 1D 13
Northwood. *IOW* 1B 40
North Wootton. *Dors* 2B 26
North Wootton. *Som* 2A 16
North Wraxall. *Wilts* 2D 7
North Wroughton. *Swin* 1C 9
Norton. *IOW* 2A 40
Norton. *W Sus* 3C 33
(nr. Arundel)
Norton. *W Sus* 1B 42
(nr. Selsey)
Norton. *Wilts* 1D 7
Norton Bavant. *Wilts* 2A 18
Norton Ferris. *Wilts* 3C 17
Norton Fitzwarren. *Som* 1B 24
Norton Green. *IOW* 2A 40
Norton Hawkfield. *Bath* 3A 6
Norton Malreward. *Bath* 3B 6
Norton St Philip. *Som* 1C 17
Norton sub Hamdon. *Som* 2D 25
Norwood Park. *Som* 3A 16
Nottington. *Dors* 2B 36
Notton. *Dors* 1B 36
Notton. *Wilts* 3A 8
Nuffield. *Oxon* 1D 11
Nunney. *Som* 2C 17
Nunton. *Wilts* 1C 29
Nursling. *Hants* 2A 30
Nursted. *W Sus* 1A 32
Nursteed. *Wilts* 3B 8
Nurston. *V Glam* 3A 4
Nutbourne. *W Sus* 3A 32
(nr. Chichester)
Nutbourne. *W Sus* 2D 33
(nr. Pulborough)
Nyetimber. *W Sus* 1B 42
Nyewood. *W Sus* 1B 32
Nynehead. *Som* 1A 24
Nyton. *W Sus* 3C 33

O

Oakdale. *Pool* 1B 38
Oake. *Som* 1A 24
Oakhanger. *Hants* 3A 22
Oakhill. *Som* 2B 16
Oakley. *Hants* 1C 21
Oakley Green. *Wind* 2C 13
Oaksey. *Wilts* 1A 8
Oakshott. *Hants* 1A 32
Oakwoodhill. *Surr* 3D 23
Oare. *W Ber* 2C 11
Oare. *Wilts* 3C 9
Oath. *Som* 1C 25
Oborne. *Dors* 2B 26
Ockham. *Surr* 1D 23
Ockley. *Surr* 2D 23
Odcombe. *Som* 2A 26
Odd Down. *Bath* 3C 7
Odiham. *Hants* 1A 22
Odstock. *Wilts* 1C 29
Offham. *W Sus* 3D 33
Offwell. *Devn* 1A 34
Ogbourne Maizey. *Wilts* 2C 9
Ogbourne St Andrew. *Wilts* 2C 9
Ogbourne St George. *Wilts* 2D 9
Okeford Fitzpaine. *Dors* 2D 27
Okus. *Swin* 1C 9
Old Alresford. *Hants* 3C 21
Old Basing. *Hants* 1D 21
Old Burghclere. *Hants* 1B 20
Oldbury-on-Severn. *S Glo* 1B 6
Oldbury on the Hill. *Glos* 1D 7
Old Dilton. *Wilts* 2D 17
Old Down. *S Glo* 1B 6
Oldford. *Som* 1C 17
Oldland. *S Glo* 2B 6
Oldmixon. *N Som* 1C 15
Old Sodbury. *S Glo* 1C 7
Old Windsor. *Wind* 2C 13
Old Woking. *Surr* 1D 23
Oliver's Battery. *Hants* 1B 30
Olveston. *S Glo* 1B 6
Onslow Village. *Surr* 2C 23
Orchard Portman. *Som* 1B 24
Orcheston. *Wilts* 2B 18
Organford. *Dors* 1A 38
Osmington. *Dors* 2C 37
Osmington Mills. *Dors* 2C 37
Osterley. *G Lon* 2D 13
Othery. *Som* 3C 15
Otterbourne. *Hants* 1B 30
Otterford. *Som* 2B 24
Otterhampton. *Som* 2B 14
Ottershaw. *Surr* 3D 13
Otterton. *Devn* 2A 34
Otterwood. *Hants* 3B 30
Ottery St Mary. *Devn* 1A 34
Outwick. *Hants* 2C 29
Over. *S Glo* 1A 6
Overcombe. *Dors* 2B 36
Over Compton. *Dors* 2A 26
Overleigh. *Som* 3D 15
Over Stowey. *Som* 3A 14
Over Stratton. *Som* 2D 25
Over Street. *Wilts* 3B 18
Overton. *Hants* 2C 21
Overtown. *Swin* 2C 9
Over Wallop. *Hants* 3D 19
Oving. *W Sus* 3C 33
Ovington. *Hants* 3C 21
Ower. *Hants* 3B 30
(nr. Holbury)
Ower. *Hants* 2A 30
(nr. Totton)
Owermoigne. *Dors* 2C 37
Owlsmoor. *Brac* 3B 12
Ownham. *W Ber* 2B 10
Owslebury. *Hants* 1C 31
Oxbridge. *Dors* 1D 35
Oxenpill. *Som* 2D 15
Oxenwood. *Wilts* 1A 20
Oxshott. *Surr* 3D 13
Ozleworth. *Glos* 1C 7

P

Packers Hill. *Dors* 2C 27
Padworth. *W Ber* 3D 11
Pagham. *W Sus* 1B 42
Palestine. *Hants* 2D 19
Paley Street. *Wind* 2B 12
Pallington. *Dors* 1C 37
Palmerstown. *V Glam* 3A 4
Pamber End. *Hants* 1D 21
Pamber Green. *Hants* 1D 21
Pamber Heath. *Hants* 3D 11
Pamphill. *Dors* 3A 28
Panborough. *Som* 2D 15
Pangbourne. *W Ber* 2D 11
Parbrook. *Som* 3A 16
Parbrook. *W Sus* 1D 33
Parc-Seymour. *Newp* 1D 5
Pardown. *Hants* 2C 21
Park Corner. *Oxon* 1D 11
Park Gate. *Hants* 3C 31
Parkhurst. *IOW* 1B 40
Parkstone. *Pool* 1B 38
Park Street. *W Sus* 3D 23
Parley Cross. *Dors* 1B 38
Parmoor. *Buck* 1A 12
Passfield. *Hants* 3B 22
Patching. *W Sus* 3D 33
Patchway. *S Glo* 1B 6
Pathe. *Som* 3C 15
Patney. *Wilts* 1B 18
Paulton. *Bath* 1B 16
Pawlett. *Som* 2C 15
Payhembury. *Devn* 3A 24
Payton. *Som* 1A 24
Peasedown St John. *Bath* 1C 17
Peasemore. *W Ber* 2B 10
Peaslake. *Surr* 2D 23
Peasmarsh. *Som* 2C 25
Peasmarsh. *Surr* 2C 23
Pedwell. *Som* 3D 15
Peel Common. *Hants* 3C 31
Penarth. *V Glam* 2A 4
Pendomer. *Som* 2A 26
Pendoylan. *V Glam* 2A 4
Pengam. *Card* 2B 4
Penhill. *Swin* 1C 9
Penhow. *Newp* 1D 5
Pen-marc. *V Glam* 3A 4
Penmark. *V Glam* 3A 4
Penn. *Buck* 1C 13
Penn. *Dors* 1C 35
Pennington. *Hants* 1A 40
Pennsylvania. *S Glo* 2C 7
Penselwood. *Som* 3C 17
Pensford. *Bath* 3B 6
Penton Mewsey. *Hants* 2A 20
Pentre-poeth. *Newp* 1B 4
Pentridge. *Dors* 2B 28
Pentwyn. *Card* 1B 4
Pentyrch. *Card* 1A 4
Pen-y-coedcae. *Rhon* 1A 4
Penyrheol. *Cphy* 1A 4
Peper Harow. *Surr* 2C 23
Perham Down. *Wilts* 2D 19
Perry Green. *Wilts* 1A 8
Perry Street. *Som* 3C 25
Pertwood. *Wilts* 3D 17
Petersfield. *Hants* 1A 32
Petersfinger. *Wilts* 1C 29
Peterstone Wentlooge. *Newp* 1B 4
Peterston-super-Ely. *V Glam* 2A 4
Petworth. *W Sus* 1C 33
Pewsey. *Wilts* 3C 9
Pheasants Hill. *Buck* 1A 12
Phoenix Green. *Hants* 1A 22
Pibsbury. *Som* 1D 25
Picket Piece. *Hants* 2A 20
Picket Post. *Hants* 3C 29
Pict's Hill. *Som* 1D 25
Piddlehinton. *Dors* 1C 37
Piddletrenthide. *Dors* 3C 27
Pidney. *Dors* 3C 27
Pightley. *Som* 3B 14
Pikeshill. *Hants* 3D 29
Pilford. *Dors* 3B 28
Pill. *N Som* 2A 6
Pilley. *Hants* 1A 40
Pillgwenlly. *Newp* 1C 5
Pill, The. *Mon* 1D 5
Pillwell. *Dors* 2C 27
Pilning. *S Glo* 1A 6
Pilsdon. *Dors* 1D 35
Pilton. *Som* 2A 16
Pimperne. *Dors* 3A 28
Pinkneys Green. *Wind* 1B 12
Pinner. *G Lon* 1D 13
Pirbright. *Surr* 1C 23
Pishill. *Oxon* 1A 12
Pitch Place. *Surr* 1C 23
Pitcombe. *Som* 3B 16
Pitminster. *Som* 2B 24
Pitney. *Som* 1D 25
Pitsford Hill. *Som* 3A 14
Pitt. *Hants* 1B 30
Pitton. *Wilts* 3D 19
Plainsfield. *Som* 3A 14
Plaistow. *W Sus* 3D 23
Plaitford. *Wilts* 2D 29
Plastow Green. *Hants* 3C 11
Play Hatch. *Oxon* 2A 12
Plush. *Dors* 3C 27
Plymtree. *Devn* 3A 24
Podimore. *Som* 1A 26
Pokesdown. *Bour* 1C 39
Poling. *W Sus* 3D 33
Poling Corner. *W Sus* 3D 33
Polsham. *Som* 2A 16
Pondtail. *Hants* 1B 22
Ponthir. *Torf* 1C 5
Pontypridd. *Rhon* 1A 4
Pontywaun. *Cphy* 1B 4
Pooksgreen. *Hants* 2A 30
Poole. *Pool* 1B 38 & 60
Poole. *Som* 1A 24
Popeswood. *Brac* 3B 12
Popham. *Hants* 2C 21
Popley. *Hants* 1D 21
Porchfield. *IOW* 1B 40
Portbury. *N Som* 2A 6
Portchester. *Hants* 3D 31
Portesham. *Dors* 2B 36
Portfield. *Som* 1D 25
Porthceri. *V Glam* 3A 4
Porthkerry. *V Glam* 3A 4
Portishead. *N Som* 2D 5
Portmore. *Hants* 1A 40
Porton. *Wilts* 3C 19
Portsea. *Port* 3D 31
Portskewett. *Mon* 1A 6
Portsmouth. *Port* 1D 41 & 57
Port Solent. *Port* 3D 31
Portswood. *Sotn* 2B 30
Post Green. *Dors* 1A 38
Potterne. *Wilts* 1A 18
Potterne Wick. *Wilts* 1A 18
Pottle Street. *Wilts* 2D 17
Poulner. *Hants* 3C 29

Turners Puddle—Whitestaunton

Turners Puddle. *Dors* ... 1D **37**
Turnworth. *Dors* ... 3D **27**
Turville. *Buck* ... 1A **12**
Turville Heath. *Buck* ... 1A **12**
Tutts Clump. *W Ber* ... 2C **11**
Twerton. *Bath* ... 3C **7**
Twinhoe. *Bath* ... 1C **17**
Twyford. *Dors* ... 2D **27**
Twyford. *Hants* ... 1B **30**
Twyford. *Wok* ... 2A **12**
Tye. *Hants* ... 3A **32**
Tyneham. *Dors* ... 2D **37**
Tytherington. *Som* ... 2C **17**
Tytherington. *S Glo* ... 1B **6**
Tytherington. *Wilts* ... 2A **18**
Tytherleigh. *Devn* ... 3C **25**

U

Ubley. *Bath* ... 1A **16**
Uffcott. *Wilts* ... 2C **9**
Uffculme. *Devn* ... 2A **24**
Uffington. *Oxon* ... 1A **10**
Ufton Nervet. *W Ber* ... 3D **11**
Ugford. *Wilts* ... 3B **18**
Ulwell. *Dors* ... 2B **38**
Undy. *Mon* ... 1D **5**
Upavon. *Wilts* ... 1C **19**
Up Cerne. *Dors* ... 3B **26**
Uphall. *Dors* ... 3A **26**
Upham. *Hants* ... 1C **31**
Uphill. *N Som* ... 1C **15**
Uploders. *Dors* ... 1A **36**
Uplyme. *Devn* ... 1C **35**
Up Marden. *W Sus* ... 2A **32**
Up Nately. *Hants* ... 1D **21**
Upottery. *Devn* ... 3B **24**
Upper Basildon. *W Ber* ... 2C **11**
Upper Bucklebury. *W Ber* ... 3C **11**
Upper Bullington. *Hants* ... 2B **20**
Upper Burgate. *Hants* ... 2C **29**
Upper Canterton. *Hants* ... 2D **29**
Upper Cheddon. *Som* ... 1B **24**
Upper Chicksgrove. *Wilts* ... 1A **28**
Upper Church Village. *Rhon* ... 1A **4**
Upper Chute. *Wilts* ... 1D **19**
Upper Clatford. *Hants* ... 2A **20**
Upper Cokeham. *W Sus* ... 3D **33**
Upper Common. *Hants* ... 2D **21**
Upper Enham. *Hants* ... 2A **20**
Upper Farringdon. *Hants* ... 3A **22**
Upper Froyle. *Hants* ... 2A **22**
Upper Godney. *Som* ... 2D **15**
Upper Green. *W Ber* ... 3A **10**
Upper Hale. *Surr* ... 2B **22**
Upper Halliford. *Surr* ... 3D **13**
Upper Kilcott. *Glos* ... 1C **7**
Upper Lambourn. *W Ber* ... 1A **10**
Upper Langford. *N Som* ... 1D **15**
Upper Minety. *Wilts* ... 1B **8**
Upper Norwood. *W Sus* ... 2C **33**
Upper Nyland. *Dors* ... 1C **27**
Upper Pennington. *Hants* ... 1A **40**
Upper Seagry. *Wilts* ... 1A **8**
Upper Street. *Hants* ... 2C **29**
Upper Studley. *Wilts* ... 1D **17**
Upperton. *W Sus* ... 1C **33**
Upper Town. *N Som* ... 3A **6**
Upper Upham. *Wilts* ... 2D **9**
Upper Wield. *Hants* ... 3D **21**
Upper Woodford. *Wilts* ... 3C **19**
Upper Wootton. *Hants* ... 1C **21**
Upper Wraxall. *Wilts* ... 2D **7**
Up Somborne. *Hants* ... 3A **20**
Up Sydling. *Dors* ... 3B **26**
Upton. *Devn* ... 3A **24**
Upton. *Dors* ... 1A **38**
(nr. Poole)
Upton. *Dors* ... 2C **37**
(nr. Weymouth)
Upton. *Hants* ... 1A **20**
(nr. Andover)
Upton. *Hants* ... 2A **30**
(nr. Southampton)
Upton. *IOW* ... 1C **41**
Upton. *Oxon* ... 1C **11**
Upton. *Slo* ... 2C **13**
Upton. *Som* ... 1D **25**
Upton. *Wilts* ... 3D **17**
Upton Cheyney. *S Glo* ... 3B **6**
Upton Grey. *Hants* ... 2D **21**
Upton Lovell. *Wilts* ... 2A **18**
Upton Noble. *Som* ... 3C **17**
Upton Scudamore. *Wilts* ... 2D **17**
Upwaltham. *W Sus* ... 2C **33**
Upwey. *Dors* ... 2B **36**
Urchfont. *Wilts* ... 1B **18**
Uxbridge. *G Lon* ... 1D **13**

V

Valley End. *Surr* ... 3C **13**
Vellow. *Som* ... 3A **14**
Venn Ottery. *Devn* ... 1A **34**
Ventnor. *IOW* ... 3C **41**
Vernham Dean. *Hants* ... 1A **20**
Vernham Street. *Hants* ... 1A **20**
Verwood. *Dors* ... 3B **28**
Vicarage. *Devn* ... 2B **34**
Virginia Water. *Surr* ... 3C **13**
Vobster. *Som* ... 2C **17**
Vole. *Som* ... 2C **15**

W

Wadbrook. *Devn* ... 3C **25**
Wadeford. *Som* ... 2C **25**
Wadswick. *Wilts* ... 3D **7**
Wadwick. *Hants* ... 1B **20**
Walberton. *W Sus* ... 3C **33**
Walcombe. *Som* ... 2A **16**
Walcot. *Swin* ... 1C **9**
Walderton. *W Sus* ... 2A **32**
Walditch. *Dors* ... 1D **35**
Walhampton. *Hants* ... 1A **40**
Walkford. *Dors* ... 1D **39**
Wallingford. *Oxon* ... 1D **11**
Wallington. *Hants* ... 3C **31**
Wallisdown. *Pool* ... 1B **38**
Walliswood. *Surr* ... 3D **23**
Walterston. *V Glam* ... 2A **4**
Waltham Chase. *Hants* ... 2C **31**
Waltham St Lawrence. *Wind* ... 2B **12**
Walton. *Som* ... 3D **15**
Walton Elm. *Dors* ... 2C **27**
Walton-in-Gordano. *N Som* ... 2D **5**
Walton-on-Thames. *Surr* ... 3D **13**
Wambrook. *Som* ... 3B **24**
Wanborough. *Surr* ... 2C **23**
Wanborough. *Swin* ... 1D **9**
Wanstrow. *Som* ... 2C **17**
Wantage. *Oxon* ... 1B **10**
Wapley. *S Glo* ... 2C **7**
Warblington. *Hants* ... 3A **32**
Wardley. *W Sus* ... 1B **32**
Wareham. *Dors* ... 2A **38**
Warfield. *Brac* ... 2B **12**
Wargrave. *Wok* ... 2A **12**
Warminghurst. *W Sus* ... 2D **33**
Warminster. *Wilts* ... 2D **17**
Warmley. *S Glo* ... 2B **6**
Warmwell. *Dors* ... 2C **37**
Warnford. *Hants* ... 1D **31**
Warningcamp. *W Sus* ... 3D **33**
Warren Corner. *Hants* ... 2B **22**
(nr. Aldershot)
Warren Corner. *Hants* ... 1A **32**
(nr. Petersfield)
Warren Row. *Wind* ... 1B **12**
Warsash. *Hants* ... 3B **30**
Wash Common. *W Ber* ... 3B **10**
Washford. *Som* ... 2A **14**
Washington. *W Sus* ... 2D **33**
Watchet. *Som* ... 2A **14**
Watchfield. *Oxon* ... 1D **9**
Waterbeach. *W Sus* ... 3B **32**
Waterditch. *Hants* ... 1C **39**
Waterlip. *Som* ... 2B **16**
Waterloo. *Cphy* ... 1A **4**
Waterloo. *Pool* ... 1B **38**
Waterlooville. *Hants* ... 3D **31**
Waterrow. *Som* ... 1A **24**
Watersfield. *W Sus* ... 2D **33**
Watton. *Dors* ... 1D **35**
Wattsville. *Cphy* ... 1B **4**
Waverley. *Surr* ... 2B **22**
Wayford. *Som* ... 3D **25**
Waytown. *Dors* ... 1D **35**
Weare. *Som* ... 1D **15**
Wearne. *Som* ... 1D **25**
Wedhampton. *Wilts* ... 1B **18**
Wedmore. *Som* ... 2D **15**
Weeke. *Hants* ... 3B **20**
Welford. *W Ber* ... 2B **10**
Well. *Hants* ... 2A **22**
Well Bottom. *Dors* ... 2A **28**
Wellhouse. *W Ber* ... 2C **11**
Wellington. *Som* ... 1A **24**
Wellow. *Bath* ... 1C **17**
Wellow. *IOW* ... 2A **40**
Wells. *Som* ... 2A **16**
Welton. *Bath* ... 1B **16**
Wembdon. *Som* ... 3B **14**
Wenvoe. *V Glam* ... 2A **4**
Wepham. *W Sus* ... 3D **33**
West Amesbury. *Wilts* ... 2C **19**
West Ashling. *W Sus* ... 3B **32**
West Ashton. *Wilts* ... 1D **17**
West Bagborough. *Som* ... 3A **14**
West Bay. *Dors* ... 1D **35**
West Bexington. *Dors* ... 2A **36**
Westbourne. *Bour* ... 1B **38**
Westbourne. *W Sus* ... 3A **32**
West Bradley. *Som* ... 3A **16**
Westbrook. *Wilts* ... 3A **8**
West Buckland. *Som* ... 1A **24**
West Burton. *W Sus* ... 2D **33**
Westbury. *Wilts* ... 1D **17**
Westbury Leigh. *Wilts* ... 2D **17**
Westbury on Trym. *Bris* ... 2A **6**
Westbury-sub-Mendip. *Som* ... 2A **16**
West Byfleet. *Surr* ... 3D **13**
West Camel. *Som* ... 1A **26**
West Chaldon. *Dors* ... 2C **37**
West Challow. *Oxon* ... 1A **10**
West Chelborough. *Dors* ... 3A **26**
West Chiltington. *W Sus* ... 2D **33**
West Chiltington Common.
W Sus ... 2D **33**
West Chinnock. *Som* ... 2D **25**
West Chisenbury. *Wilts* ... 1C **19**
West Clandon. *Surr* ... 1D **23**
West Coker. *Som* ... 2A **26**
Westcombe. *Som* ... 3B **16**
(nr. Evercreech)
Westcombe. *Som* ... 1D **25**
(nr. Somerton)
West Compton. *Dors* ... 1A **36**
West Compton. *Som* ... 2A **16**
Westcot. *Oxon* ... 1A **10**
Westcott. *Surr* ... 2D **23**
West Cranmore. *Som* ... 2B **16**
West Dean. *W Sus* ... 2B **32**
West Dean. *Wilts* ... 1D **29**
West Drayton. *G Lon* ... 2D **13**
West End. *Dors* ... 3A **28**
West End. *Hants* ... 2B **30**
West End. *N Som* ... 3D **5**
West End. *S Glo* ... 1C **7**
West End. *Surr* ... 3C **13**
West End. *Wilts* ... 1A **28**
West End. *Wind* ... 2B **12**
West End Green. *Hants* ... 3D **11**
Westergate. *W Sus* ... 3C **33**
Westerleigh. *S Glo* ... 2B **6**
Westerton. *W Sus* ... 3B **32**
Westfields. *Dors* ... 3C **27**
Westford. *Som* ... 2A **24**
West Ginge. *Oxon* ... 1B **10**
West Grafton. *Wilts* ... 3D **9**
West Green. *Hants* ... 1A **22**
West Grimstead. *Wilts* ... 1D **29**
West Hagbourne. *Oxon* ... 1C **11**
Westham. *Dors* ... 3B **36**
Westham. *Som* ... 2D **15**
Westhampnett. *W Sus* ... 3B **32**
West Hanney. *Oxon* ... 1B **10**
West Harnham. *Wilts* ... 1C **29**
West Harptree. *Bath* ... 1A **16**
West Harting. *W Sus* ... 1A **32**
West Hatch. *Som* ... 1B **24**
Westhay. *Som* ... 2D **15**
West Heath. *Hants* ... 1C **21**
(nr. Basingstoke)
West Heath. *Hants* ... 1B **22**
(nr. Farnborough)
West Hendred. *Oxon* ... 1B **10**
West Hewish. *N Som* ... 3C **5**
West Hill. *Devn* ... 1A **34**
West Hill. *N Som* ... 2D **5**
West Holme. *Dors* ... 2D **37**
West Horrington. *Som* ... 2A **16**
West Horsley. *Surr* ... 1D **23**
West Howe. *Bour* ... 1B **38**
West Huntspill. *Som* ... 2C **15**
West Hyde. *Herts* ... 1D **13**
West Ilsley. *W Ber* ... 1B **10**
West Itchenor. *W Sus* ... 3B **32**
West Kennett. *Wilts* ... 3C **9**
West Kington. *Wilts* ... 2D **7**
West Knighton. *Dors* ... 2C **37**
West Knoyle. *Wilts* ... 3D **17**
West Lambrook. *Som* ... 2D **25**
West Lavington. *W Sus* ... 1B **32**
West Lavington. *Wilts* ... 1B **18**
Westleigh. *Devn* ... 2A **24**
West Littleton. *S Glo* ... 2C **7**
West Lulworth. *Dors* ... 2D **37**
West Lydford. *Som* ... 3A **16**
West Lyng. *Som* ... 1C **25**
West Marden. *W Sus* ... 2A **32**
West Meon. *Hants* ... 1D **31**
West Milton. *Dors* ... 1A **36**
West Molesey. *Surr* ... 3D **13**
West Monkton. *Som* ... 1B **24**
West Moors. *Dors* ... 3B **28**
West Morden. *Dors* ... 1A **38**
West Newton. *Som* ... 1B **24**
Weston. *Bath* ... 3C **7**
Weston. *Devn* ... 3A **24**
(nr. Honiton)
Weston. *Devn* ... 2A **34**
(nr. Sidmouth)
Weston. *Dors* ... 3B **36**
(nr. Weymouth)
Weston. *Dors* ... 3A **26**
(nr. Yeovil)
Weston. *Hants* ... 1A **32**
Weston. *W Ber* ... 2A **10**
Weston Bampfylde. *Som* ... 1B **26**
Westonbirt. *Glos* ... 1D **7**
Weston-in-Gordano. *N Som* ... 2D **5**
Weston Patrick. *Hants* ... 2D **21**
Weston-super-Mare. *N Som* ... 3C **5**
Weston Town. *Som* ... 2C **17**
Westonzoyland. *Som* ... 3C **15**
West Orchard. *Dors* ... 2D **27**
West Overton. *Wilts* ... 3C **9**
West Parley. *Dors* ... 1B **38**
West Pennard. *Som* ... 3A **16**
Westport. *Som* ... 2C **25**
West Quantoxhead. *Som* ... 2A **14**
Westra. *V Glam* ... 2A **4**
West Stafford. *Dors* ... 2C **37**
West Stoke. *W Sus* ... 3B **32**
West Stoughton. *Som* ... 2D **15**
West Stour. *Dors* ... 1C **27**
West Stowell. *Wilts* ... 3C **9**
West Stratton. *Hants* ... 2C **21**
West Thorney. *W Sus* ... 3A **32**
West Tisted. *Hants* ... 1D **31**
West Town. *Bath* ... 3A **6**
West Town. *Hants* ... 1A **42**
West Town. *N Som* ... 3D **5**
West Tytherley. *Hants* ... 1D **29**
West Tytherton. *Wilts* ... 2A **8**
West Wellow. *Hants* ... 2D **29**
West Wick. *N Som* ... 3C **5**
West Winterslow. *Wilts* ... 3D **19**
West Wittering. *W Sus* ... 1A **42**
Westwood. *Wilts* ... 1D **17**
West Woodhay. *W Ber* ... 3A **10**
West Woodlands. *Som* ... 2C **17**
West Worldham. *Hants* ... 3A **22**
West Worthing. *W Sus* ... 3D **33**
West Yatton. *Wilts* ... 2D **7**
Wexcombe. *Wilts* ... 1D **19**
Wexham Street. *Buck* ... 1C **13**
Weybourne. *Surr* ... 2B **22**
Weybridge. *Surr* ... 3D **13**
Weycroft. *Devn* ... 1C **35**
Weyhill. *Hants* ... 2A **20**
Weymouth. *Dors* ... 3B **36**
Whaddon. *Wilts* ... 1C **29**
Whatley. *Som* ... 3C **25**
(nr. Chard)
Whatley. *Som* ... 2C **17**
(nr. Frome)
Wheatley. *Hants* ... 2A **22**
Wheelerstreet. *Surr* ... 2C **23**
Wherwell. *Hants* ... 2A **20**
Whimple. *Devn* ... 1A **34**
Whippingham. *IOW* ... 1C **41**
Whistley Green. *Wok* ... 2A **12**
Whitchurch. *Bath* ... 3B **6**
Whitchurch. *Card* ... 2A **4**
Whitchurch. *Hants* ... 2B **20**
Whitchurch Canonicorum. *Dors* ... 1C **35**
Whitchurch Hill. *Oxon* ... 2D **11**
Whitchurch-on-Thames. *Oxon* ... 2D **11**
Whitcombe. *Dors* ... 2C **37**
Whitefield. *Dors* ... 1A **38**
Whitefield. *Som* ... 1A **24**
Whitehall. *Devn* ... 2A **24**
Whitehall. *Hants* ... 1A **22**
Whitehall. *W Sus* ... 1D **33**
Whitehill. *Hants* ... 3A **22**
White Lackington. *Dors* ... 1C **37**
Whitelackington. *Som* ... 2C **25**
Whiteley. *Hants* ... 2C **31**
Whiteley Bank. *IOW* ... 2C **41**
Whiteley Village. *Surr* ... 3D **13**
Whitenap. *Hants* ... 1A **30**
Whiteparish. *Wilts* ... 1D **29**
Whitestaunton. *Som* ... 2B **24**

Every possible care has been taken to ensure that, to the best of our knowledge, the information contained in this atlas is accurate at the date of publication. However, we cannot warrant that our work is entirely error free and whilst we would be grateful to learn of any inaccuracies, we do not accept any responsibility for loss or damage resulting from reliance on information contained within this publication.

The representation on the maps of a road, track or footpath is no evidence of the existence of a right of way.

The Grid on this map is the National Grid taken from Ordnance Survey® mapping with the permission of the Controller of Her Majesty's Stationery Office.

SAFETY CAMERA INFORMATION

Safety camera locations are publicised by the Safer Roads Partnership who operate them in order to encourage drivers to comply with speed limits at these sites. It is the driver's absolute responsibility to be aware of and to adhere to speed limits at all times.

By showing this safety camera information it is the intention of Geographers' A-Z Map Company Ltd., to encourage safe driving and greater awareness of speed limits and vehicle speed. Data accurate at time of printing.

CITY & TOWN CENTRE PLANS

Reference to Town Plans

MOTORWAY	M3
MOTORWAY UNDER CONSTRUCTION	
MOTORWAY PROPOSED	
MOTORWAY JUNCTIONS WITH NUMBERS	4 5
Unlimited Interchange	4
Limited Interchange	5
PRIMARY ROUTE	A33
DUAL CARRIAGEWAYS	A30
CLASS A ROAD	
CLASS B ROAD	B2070
MAJOR ROADS UNDER CONSTRUCTION	
MAJOR ROADS PROPOSED	
MINOR ROADS	
RESTRICTED ACCESS	
PEDESTRIANIZED ROAD & MAIN FOOTWAY	
ONE WAY STREETS	
TOLL	TOLL
RAILWAY AND STATION	
UNDERGROUND / METRO & DLR STATION	DLR
LEVEL CROSSING AND TUNNEL	
TRAM STOP AND ONE WAY TRAM STOP	
BUILT-UP AREA	
ABBEY, CATHEDRAL, PRIORY ETC.	†

BUS STATION	
CAR PARK (Selection of)	P
CHURCH	†
CITY WALL	
FERRY (Vehicular)	
(Foot only)	
GOLF COURSE	
HELIPORT	
HOSPITAL	H
INFORMATION CENTRE	i
LIGHTHOUSE	
MARKET	
NATIONAL TRUST PROPERTY (Open)	NT
(Restricted opening)	NT
PARK & RIDE	P+⊕
PLACE OF INTEREST	■
POLICE STATION	▲
POST OFFICE	★
SHOPPING AREA (Main street and precinct)	
SHOPMOBILITY	
TOILET	▽
VIEWPOINT	

BATH

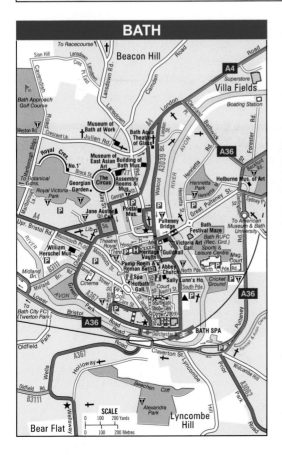

BOURNEMOUTH

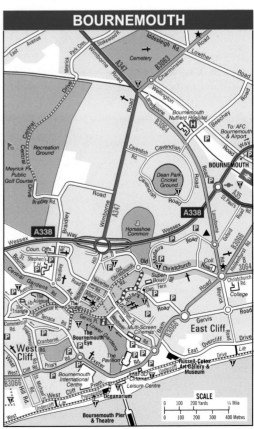

BRISTOL

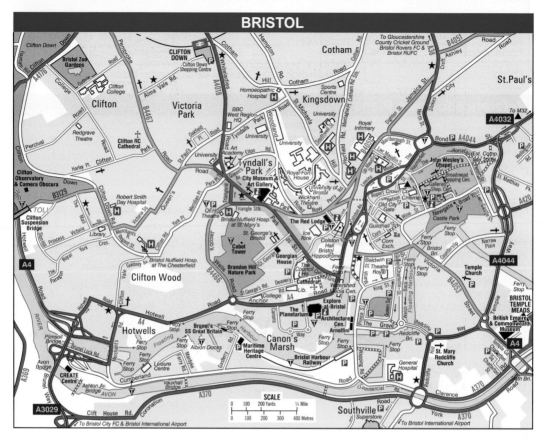

CARDIFF (CAERDYDD)

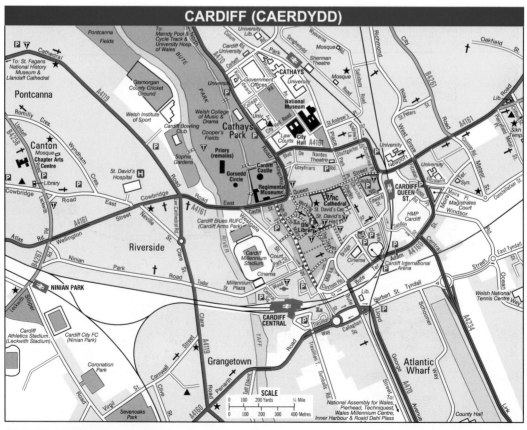

GUILDFORD

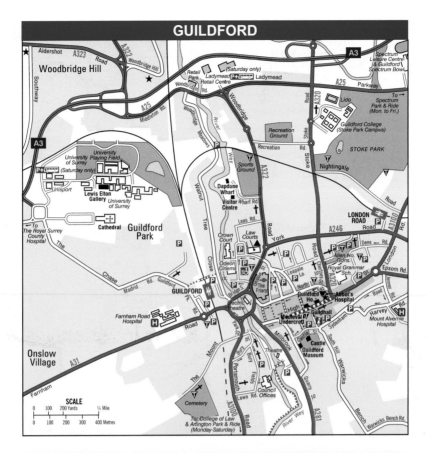

PORTSMOUTH

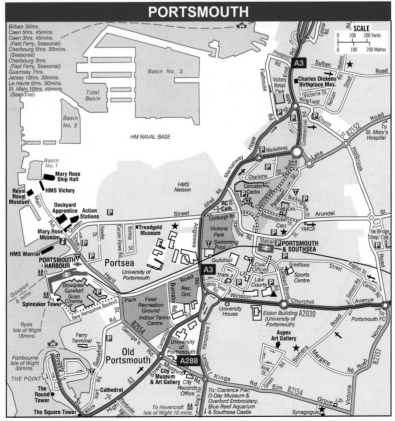

READING

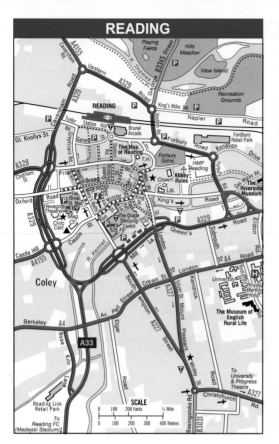

SALISBURY

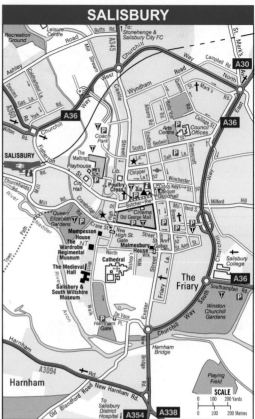

SOUTHAMPTON

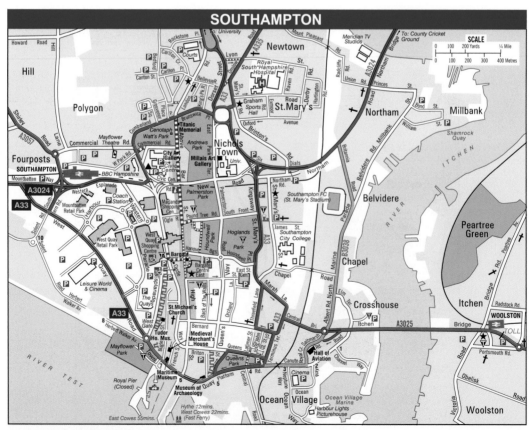

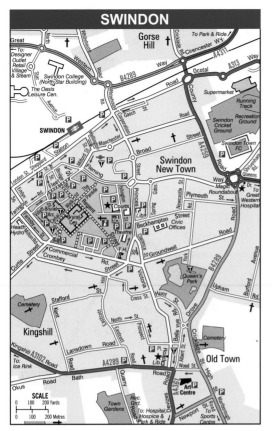

SWINDON

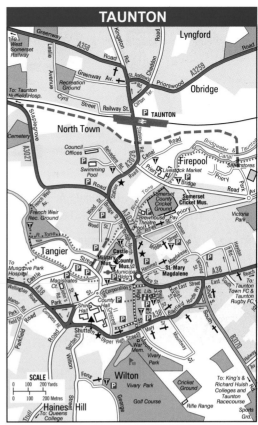

TAUNTON

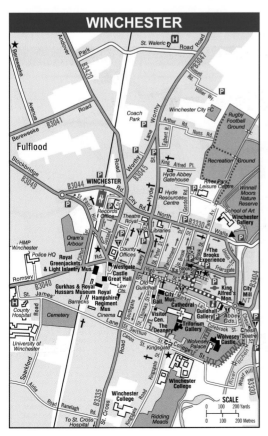

WINCHESTER

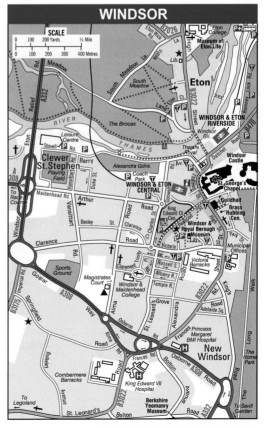

WINDSOR

LONDON HEATHROW

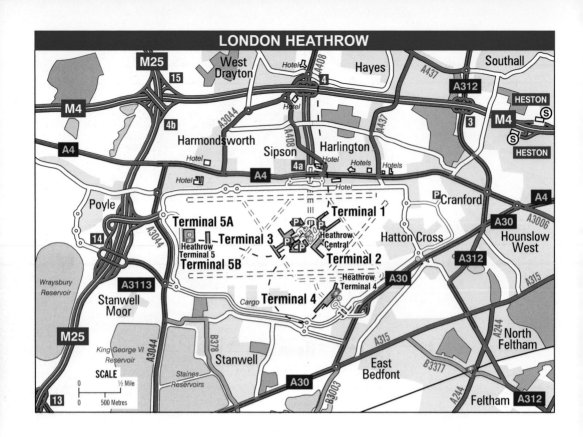

POOLE

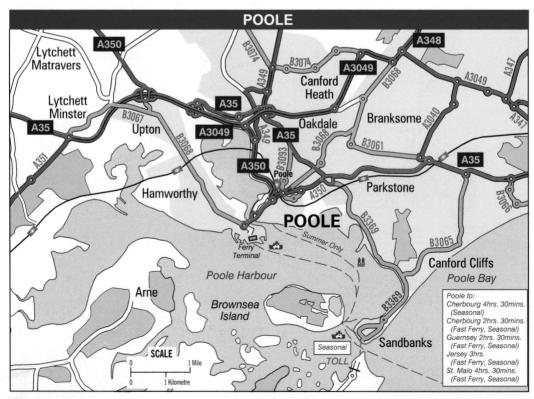

Poole to:
Cherbourg 4hrs. 30mins.
  (Seasonal)
Cherbourg 2hrs. 30mins.
  (Fast Ferry, Seasonal)
Guernsey 2hrs. 30mins.
  (Fast Ferry, Seasonal)
Jersey 3hrs.
  (Fast Ferry, Seasonal)
St. Malo 4hrs. 30mins.
  (Fast Ferry, Seasonal)